Who Are the
CHRISTIANS
in the
CHURCH?

How Do You Know?

Lorraine McCullough-Brown

ISBN 979-8-89112-402-8 (Paperback)
ISBN 979-8-89112-404-2 (Hardcover)
ISBN 979-8-89112-403-5 (Digital)

Copyright © 2024 Lorraine McCullough-Brown
All rights reserved
First Edition

All rights reserved. No part of this publication may be reproduced, distributed, or transmitted in any form or by any means, including photocopying, recording, or other electronic or mechanical methods without the prior written permission of the publisher. For permission requests, solicit the publisher via the address below.

Covenant Books
11661 Hwy 707
Murrells Inlet, SC 29576
www.covenantbooks.com

Special dedication to five godly influential women in my life: my mother, Sadie L. McCullough; mother-in-love, Mrs. Lillie L. Brown; ministers' spouses, ladies Catherine Mayfield Maness and Delois Woody Walker; and Mrs. Minnie Crowder, whom I met when I became a CME at an early age in Monroe, North Carolina.

In loving memory of my mother—Sadie Lois Gibson McCullough

Mama, I feel that you are still by my side. I miss our funny conversations, especially when you say that I am talking crazy. You were a tough and beautiful godly woman. You raised all of us to understand the power of hard work and gratitude. I followed your teachings every day of my life. Yes, some days, I missed the mark but I know that you knew I wasn't perfect. I know now that if I put in the time and effort, everything I aim for, I will get. I possess the same strength and internal force as you. You were and are still my rock in the storm, along with God. Thanks for being my most beloved companion. I love and miss you so much. I thank God that He allowed me to be your daughter.

As Shirley Caesar said in her song, "I remember Mama in a special way." Your passing was so unexpected for me. I miss having you to talk to when I become overwhelmed. Only you knew what was happening to me. I talk to your pictures beside my bed. Believe it or not, I still say some of the silly things that would make you laugh. To some, it may sound silly, but you and one other family member were the only ones who really knew me and how and why I struggled with balancing the *why*s of life. I tell you how my day was, whether good or bad. I love and miss you, Mama. I remember when you had to put a flower on one of your sons' grave and how hard it is for a mother to do it. Mama, it's just as hard for a child to place flowers on their mama's grave. I still hold our memories close to my heart. MISS YOU! By the way, I am using my mouth to write words to inspire and encourage others who may have experienced some of the same habits I possessed.

In loving memory of someone special—Catherine Maness

Saying *thank you* is a small word because, when I was in your presence or sharing many pleasant conversations on the phone, you taught me that just being myself was the best way for people to love and learn who I really am. You were a great supporter of my leadership as president of the Carolina Regional Ministers' Spouses. It pleased me so much when you and Elder Maness drove in heavy rain from Georgia to Parkwood CME Church in Charlotte for a ministers' spouses workshop. It touched me greatly to see you, knowing you were facing health challenges, but your smile showed a woman with strong strength of character. *You were someone special, someone set apart, and your memories will last forever engraved upon my heart.*

In loving memory of my historian—Minnie Crowder

I treasure many of the conversations we shared when I first moved to Monroe, North Carolina. It's an honor that you would ask Jack and me to stay with you when your daughter had to go out of town. I would try to convince you that Jack didn't need to come with me, but I realized he was the one who would keep her laughing and could share a lot more information about the history of the CME Church. (She loved history.)

I called her my historian because she would tell me things about Monroe and family connections. She shared how she and another teacher were chosen to start teaching at a White school because of the color of their skin. But she said she let it be known that she still expected to be respected. She said many of the White students didn't know that she was "colored." Well, we know how they learned the difference.

I remembered how she trusted my driving to pick up her daughter for choir rehearsal. We laughed because she said (her daughter) she had never seen a person as short as me driving such a big car so fast, especially when I would turn into a curve so fast that all the kids in the back seat would roll to one big pile in the back (BUT GOD). I was in my early twenties and on the move. I enjoyed how she shared the changes in the locations of annual conferences from the churches and how they really changed the atmosphere of the conferences. I never would have known or thought your daughter would be my boss. Thank God I didn't wreck and left a scar on her because she might have used it as my having poor judgment (ha ha). But I praise and thank God that she still treats me with high respect. It's because of the teaching from a loving and caring mother. I do miss the laughter, but the memories are keepsakes. I will never part with them. God has you in His keeping, and I have you in my heart.

In loving memory—Mrs. Lillie Lue Sanders Brown

In loving memory of an earth angel, my mother-in-love, Lillie Brown. I was blessed to have you in my life. I was even more blessed when you gave me a warm hug when you were told that I was going to be your daughter-in-law, and you said, "Welcome! Welcome! Welcome!" You reminded me so much of my mother. I could sense your caring and loving spirit while you were holding me so close to your heart. You both loved the Lord and would do whatever you could to help and bless others. God knew that I was a "mama's girl, and I needed someone with true "mother love," so He placed me in your life. I will always cherish how you loved and accepted me. You were so selfless and thoughtful, and you put love into everything you did. That's why so many people loved you.

The Saturday before you passed, you were preparing food in case company came by and wanted to eat, not knowing that it would be the last big Sunday dinner. I will always cherish your love and the memories we shared together.

In honor of a very special friendship—Lady Delois W. Walker

You never know how special you are to me. The saying that opposite attracts—well, I can say that is us. I am a talker, and you are a quiet listener. I find your friendship a special gift. It is often said that a friend is a gift one often gives themselves. Your friendship exemplifies what a friend really is because you are constantly giving of yourself quietly.

Introduction

This book tells what God's words really meant versus what I was told. It tells how, as a child, I received mixed information about what God's word really meant in the Bible. As a child, it seemed that there were categories for sins based on what act a person performed. The reason I was led to believe that there were categories was that what I was told was different from what I witnessed.

For some of you who have experienced some of the same contradictory teachings of God's Word, I pray that this book, *Who Are the Christians in the Church? How Do You Know?* will help clear things up for you. Many times, we have heard it said, "Can I get a witness?" But as a child, if I thought I wouldn't get beaten down, I wondered if they really wanted someone or even me to say what I really witnessed.

This book was written as a therapeutic process. To some, it may sound funny, and to others, it may be disturbing. Some may find it offensive, but *it's my life story* of the emotional challenges I faced and some I still face. As the lay ministry leader of my church, I asked a licensed professional to host a mental health workshop. She is a PK (preacher kid). One of the differences she expounded on was issues, especially in African American churches where many feel all a person needs to do is pray and give it to God. She made it known in her presentation that she told her mother that she needed counseling, and her mother wanted to know why, and she said that all she needed was to pray and give it to God.

In this book, I will share some of the barriers I faced that she mentioned, and those that prevented me from getting professional help from a licensed professional counselor.

The hardest chapter that I wrote and dealt with was "Becoming a Minister's Spouse" and how it put me in a different arena in the church, how I struggled the first year as a spouse, how I witnessed injustice from the actions of the higher and the Higher (the Elders and the Bishops during my early years as a spouse), and the hurt from *some* of my siblings and family members. There may be some who want to judge me by what I have written, but remember that this is *my story*. Before judging, know this: *"No one has the right to judge you, because no one really knows what you have been through. They might have heard the stories, but they didn't feel what you felt in your heart."* A friendly reminder of the words of Matthew 7:1–7 (KJV):

> *Judge not, that ye be not judged. For with what judgment ye judge, ye shall be judged: and with what measure ye mete, it shall be measured to you again. And why beholdest thou the mote that is in thy brother's eye, but considerest not the beam that is in thine own eye? Or how wilt thou say to thy brother, let me pull out the mote out of thine eye, and behold a beam is in thine own eye? Thou hypocrite, first cast out the beam out of thine own eye; and then shalt thou see clearly to cast out the mote of thou brother's eye.*

A better understanding of the mote is a fault one has, but we tend to ignore a greater fault of our own. JUST SAYING!

When I decided to put myself out there, I prayed to God for courage and the ability to say the truth. I will be sharing in my book, *Who Are the Christians in the Church? How Do You Know?*, some of my most hurtful events and disappointments from those who are so close to me as well as those who label themselves as Christians. This book is in no way meant to throw anyone under the bus or at the foot of the cross. Being in great standing with God as Christians, we have to be genuine and not pretentious. It's my prayer that we remember that we are all made in God's image, yet we are still different. We have to learn to respect one another and understand that we aren't going to see life from the same view, but we should acknowledge that these differences do exist. With these differences, one qualification of a Christian will not change, and that is LOVE.

At the end of the book, there will be a self-evaluation based on what a Christian life is and the expectations of a Christian. The questions will strictly come from the Bible and reflect on Jesus, Paul's teaching, and Micah chapter 6. It's designed to see that if you were honest with yourselves, could you stand up because you are a Christian? No one will be grading your response except God.

Remember this statement: *A blossom cannot tell what becomes of its fragrance as it drifts away. Just as you cannot tell what becomes of your influence as you continue through life (author unknown).*

GOD BLESS!

The Unbalanced Scale of a Christian Life as a Youth

At the age of ten, I remember as a young child how the Sunday school teachers taught the Ten Commandments. I understood what some of them meant. I just memorized the others without any knowledge of what they meant. The ones I remembered were as follows:

- Thou shalt not steal.
- Thou should honor your mother and father (I knew that meant to obey them).
- Thou shall not commit murder.
- Thou should not commit adultery (this word stood out because I didn't really know what it meant, so I became curious and decided to try to find it in the dictionary).

In my home as a child, there were several subjects not discussed around us. These subjects were sex, homosexuality (of course, we used the word *sissy* for males that act like females), and, of course, girls' monthly periods. (My mother's mom passed away during her teenage years. My mother was the oldest of four children and had to take on the role of mother figure for one of her sisters and her only brother. The youngest sister was too young for my mother to raise, so she was raised by their uncle and aunt.)

One Sunday, while studying the Ten Commandments in Sunday school, the word *adultery* stood out because the teacher tried not to explain what that commandment meant. When asked, she said that's when people aren't being nice, and she was anxious to move on to another commandment. She wouldn't answer the question when asked for examples of adultery. Well, you know the old saying, "It's always one in the crowd." In this crowd, it was two of us who kept asking why she couldn't give us an example. One thing in my favor during that era was that I didn't have a cell phone because I would've googled *adultery* and told her what I learned from Google. And a Stanley hairbrush would've been waiting for me when I arrived home from church.

As I stated in another chapter, my mother used the wood handle of a Stanley hairbrush to spank or whip us. When I got home from church, I looked up the definition of *adultery* in the dictionary. I decided to ask my mama what is so secretive about adultery and why adults make it sound so bad. She reminded me that I was the only child she had who questioned almost everything I saw or heard. Well, my smart mouth and I said, "How am I going to learn if I don't ask questions for understanding?" It appeared that it was a hush-hush word, and she didn't feel comfortable talking to me about it. She questioned why I wanted to know what it meant and why I was concerned.

My mom was a PK (a.k.a. preacher kid). I explained that Pastor Rev. Martin of Mount Sinai Baptist Church, in Mount Holly, North Carolina, where I was born, preached about adultery today, and I knew some people who fell into the category of some of the things he was saying. Of course, at ten, I cautiously said I knew some people who were doing adultery, and he called it a sin. The conversation came to a quick halt, like slamming on the car brakes *really* hard. I guess you caught my drift. She told me, "I am surprised that you even paid any attention to the sermon because you tend to hear only what you want to hear." No, I didn't get an answer, and the conversation came to an end.

Now that I am grown, I feel comfortable saying she knew that I knew what I was talking about. The reason my mom didn't know what the pastor preached was that we didn't attend the same church. The adults attended the church where my grandfather, Rev. Ferdinand Gibson, was the pastor at Bethel Baptist Church in my hometown too. There wasn't enough room in the car for the children

WHO ARE THE CHRISTIANS IN THE CHURCH?

to ride with them. The church wasn't within walking distance for us to attend with them.

Through elementary school, first to eighth grades, I attended Rock Grove African Methodist Episcopal (AME) Zion Church. Since then, the name had been changed a few times, which was about a mile from our house. My sisters JoAnn and Cynthia, my niece Ann Foxx (who lived with us), and I walked to church. That was where my father attended church when he was in town from his job.

He worked with a construction company that traveled a lot. One winter, we had an ice storm. I was the only one who was prepared to go to church, so I caught a ride with my neighbor. When we arrived at my church, the doors were locked, and no one was there. She asked if I wanted to go with her to her church, Mount Sinai Baptist Church, which was in the same neighborhood. Of course, I said yes. When the pastor asked if there were any visitors, I stood up, gave them my name, and sat back down beside my cousins Irma and Geraldine, who attended that church. Then he asked if there was anyone who wanted to join the church to come up front. So I went to the front and was introduced as a new member of Mount Sinai Baptist Church. After being introduced as the new member of the church, it was time for the pastor to preach.

When the pastor gave the title of his sermon, "The Sin of Adultery," it caught my attention. This was one of the many Sundays the ushers didn't have to tell us to be quiet. (It seems as though in all churches during that era, the ushers would make sure you weren't out of order or too loud.) I sat there quietly, like a mouse in the church, listening to what he was saying. Of course, there were some things I didn't understand, but I did hear him clearly when he gave examples of adultery.

My stomach felt like it had a knot in it. I didn't want to believe that I knew some adults who were committing *that* sin, especially when they tried to teach us to do right. It's hard to think that someone who appeared to be so humble would commit a sin and be comfortable doing it.

As a child, I didn't know there weren't categories for sin. I really thought there were good and bad things and did not look at them as sins. There is a saying that when a person is accused of doing something out of the ark of the covenant of God, they will ask, "Can you put your hands on them at that moment?" That means, "Were you there?" If I were asked that question at the time when it occurred, I could answer yes because I was there in the midst. To be careful about what I'm talking about, I am limiting and not expounding on the particular situation. I can say it was to appear to be just being neighborly. This is how the sin categories come about. (LOL.)

I lived in a home where we weren't exposed to a lot of outside gossip, at least not from our parents. I didn't hear my parents say negative things about anyone, even if they knew what was happening around the neighborhood. My mama knew things in the neighborhood, but she never talked to us about them. She encouraged us to keep our mouths shut and not repeat negative things others would say. Of course, we didn't bring them up in her presence, and perhaps I should say in no other adult presence.

In those days, many families believed in the *African proverb that says, "It takes a village to raise a child."* If we were caught gossiping and another adult heard it, well, you know the results. Sometimes, it's the severity of what we say or do that determines our punishment. It could be two whippings or two lectures. Both of them got on my nerves. Well, I knew the commandment about honoring our parents, and I am sure when they said not to "repass gossip," I knew that was a command. Even more surprising about gossiping is that I thought it was not nice but not a sin.

We can't justify sin. Sin is sin. It's like saying someone is a "little pregnant." Either you are or you aren't. If we aren't careful when someone comes to us with gossip and we allow them to continue repeating it, we are just as guilty as them.

James 4:11 states,

> *Brothers and sisters, do not slander one another. Anyone who speaks against a brother or sister or judge them speaks against the law and judges. When you judge the law, you are not keeping it, but sitting in judgement on it.*

WHO ARE THE CHRISTIANS IN THE CHURCH?

Another one that caught my eye is from *James 1:26*,

> *Those who consider themselves religious and yet do not keep a tight rein on their tongues deceive themselves, and their religion is worthless.*

As children, we were told what and what not to do but were never given a scripture, and in most cases, we didn't have Bible study time at home or joint prayer except over a meal.

Even at an early age, I learned that what some people confessed and what they did were two different things. It was very confusing to me to hear one thing and see another action. I expected adults to be honest and not sinful. Adults should want to earn youths' respect.

When people say they are Christians, I expect their actions and words to line up with the Bible and God's word. I was so confused and full of questions, but I know that if I had asked how these adults could commit what I've learned was a sin and still claim to be Christians, my mother might have whipped me with the wrong end of that Stanley hairbrush. I would probably still have marks on me from that beating. I just lived confused. So when I went to church, it didn't matter what was preached because, if I didn't understand it, I didn't feel comfortable asking the point of the sermon. When asked, I would say, "I have no idea." My mother asked whether I did not pay attention, and I just shrugged my shoulders because I didn't dare tell her the truth. No!

Going to church in high school was just a custom we followed on Sundays. The only book of the New Testament I recall hearing sermons from was Matthew. At that time of my life, if I had known what was in the book of James, I might have been convicted, especially *James 3:1–10*. That chapter really breaks down how dangerous a tongue is. I really needed to know the breakdown of a dangerous tongue. Now I am not saying that I would have changed immediately, but I would have known that I couldn't praise God and curse someone with the same tongue.

Let me say that since I didn't try learning on my own, I missed a lot by not reading for my own knowledge and understanding. I was grown when I was really introduced to the New Testament, and I was a parent. I didn't know there was a scripture commanding me to study the Bible for my own understanding. I thought it was the preacher's responsibility to teach us Bible study or, from their sermons, God's expectation of us. Woe is me!

When I graduated from high school and went to North Carolina Central University in Durham, North Carolina (NCCU), going to church was a lost cause. As a freshman, I had to attend Vesper Services on campus every Sunday. When I moved to the next level as a sophomore, I got up for breakfast, waited for lunch, and picked up a snack bag for dinner. I didn't go to Vespers. I later learned, years after leaving Durham, that there was a CME church down the street from the men's dormitory. I don't know if it was against the university's policy for churches to invite students to their churches. I might or might not have gone. Oh, well, that's water under the bridge.

In support of my lack of knowledge, I will quote a statement from Maya Angelou: *"Do the best you can until you know better. Then when you know better, do better."*

When I Became a Teenager

When I became a teenager, I had the impression that I was ready to have a boyfriend. Society can take some credit for that assumption. When young girls or older girls reach a certain age, they are looked at as if they have a problem if they aren't interested in boys. They will call you a "tomboy" or a "butch" (the term used now is *lesbian*).

I was thirteen years old and in my first year of high school when I had a boyfriend. He was a sophomore, and that went over like a lead balloon with my mom. She knew I wasn't ready for a boyfriend because I was still young at heart and very naive. One thing she was concerned about was the fact that I didn't know him, and of course, she didn't know him or his family. I laughed a lot with him, but we only saw each other at school and maybe sometimes talked on the phone. Unfortunately, that didn't last long because he was killed in a car accident on a very rainy and stormy day. I did miss him and the laughter, but we weren't in a relationship where I lost sleep and couldn't continue my life journey at thirteen. Needless to say, I didn't consider another boyfriend until the second semester of my sophomore year of high school. We dated for several years, even in college. Trust me, it wasn't smooth sailing the whole time.

If you are in or have been in a relationship and you can tell time by the way he or she spends it with you, then it all changes with excuses why they aren't available. READ THE WRITING ON THE WALL. That statement came from the fifth chapter of Daniel. I am sure you are aware of that story.

So this is how I see the correlation between Belshazzar, his nobles, his wives, and his concubine. My boyfriend was popular. He was well-known, liked to dress well, and always tried to impress people by saying cute little phrases. I was known as his girlfriend throughout the school. Even the principal thought we spent too much time together. He, the principal, went so far as to tell me that every year since he was principal at the school, someone at the top of the senior's class wouldn't get to march with their graduating class because they were pregnant, and he said he thought I would be that person. (During that era of my life, if you were pregnant, you were treated like you had a plague and were ousted from school, but you could receive your diploma.) He may have been correct about a situation that would've disallowed me from marching with my classmates, but it surely would not have been because of pregnancy but because of what was about to roll off of my "dangerous tongue."

My thoughts and the words I spoke at that time would not have been acceptable to God. I would have said some awful, demeaning, and insulting words to him, and that would've been the reason I could've been kicked out of the school system in the Gaston County area. God, I thank You for holding my tongue. I was so upset that my jaws and tongue felt glued together. I could only give him a very mean look, and I walked away. I know it wasn't because I was so holy that I put a bridle on my own tongue because I wasn't known for holding my peace. Little did he know that I was very naive about sex.

I was still playing with paper dolls, and I received my last doll in the eleventh grade. Needless to say, you can see why the third wheel came into play. When I arrived home from school, I told my mama what the principal said. She called school the next day and gently expressed her dislike of what he said to me. He apologized to her, and when he tried to do the same with me, I just looked and tightly kept my mouth shut. I do know my mama would not approve of what was on my mind at that moment, nor would God be pleased. Even Belshazzar received messages from God that appeared on the wall, and he couldn't understand them, so he hired many people to translate.

As I stated earlier, I started noticing the changes. I mentioned it to a close friend. I guess you might say I should've noticed something was going on. Like Belshazzar, he couldn't understand what the writing was saying. I had no reason, I thought, not to trust him because we were together at school and she saw us. Well, she knew I was his girlfriend, and she was happy being the concubine.

The role of the concubines was simple during biblical times. They were there in the case of a barren wife (one who couldn't provide children and also provide male sexual desires). There was no way on this side of God's kingdom was I not able to bear it. I didn't want to bear, nor was I interested in trying to bear.

When I asked my friend, Wayne Farrar, he knew what was going on, and he said he wanted to tell me but was afraid it would cause a problem with our friendship since we had been friends since elementary school. He stated he tried throwing hints, but I seemed to be oblivious to what he was saying. That's why he backed out until he felt guilty and took a chance, telling me again and straight to the point.

He told me why he wasn't coming on Sundays like clockwork and why sometimes he would come by so late. It was because he was going where he could get what wasn't available by being with me. When he would come by, he would make up a lie, stating he was waiting for his ride. The concubine (as I am comparing it with Belshazzar's situation) was two years younger than us. My friend Wayne interpreted the writing on the wall for me, stating he drove my boyfriend to see her. Of course, when I asked him about it, he denied it. He never took ownership of the truth. As my mama would say, "Lies have long legs. They will catch up with you."

I am glad to say that even in the midst of lies and betrayal, I was not, nor did I become, a prisoner of love or lack thereof. To be honest, our relationship was a mismatched situation because we were basically on different paths for our future. Sexuality was lacking, and it wasn't a need or a desire for me. I had matured enough by my senior year to know what the results could be if that was what a relationship required. Staying in a bad relationship isn't healthy for anyone, and I didn't want that for me. When I spoke of a prisoner of love, that is someone who knows that there's dishonesty, and you find yourself on an emotional roller coaster, but because of low self-esteem, you just endure and eventually experience hate and continue accepting the excuses and lies. That didn't happen to me. I got more pleasure from playing with my designer doll and dressing my paper dolls than dealing with a liar.

I learned to love myself, and I broke those chains that could have trapped me in a dead-end relationship or, more so, a dead situation. I DID IT. Don't be the third wheel or follow the example of the concubine, who never really gets recognition as someone very special in a king's life.

The third wheel in our relationship was left with a responsibility to care for and not getting the attention anymore. Nor was that little responsibility ever owned or acknowledged. A classmate informed him of what he left behind, and he denied any knowledge of it. He was then reminded that he knew what he was involved in before leaving for college.

One of my mother's famous sayings was, *"Lies have long legs. They will catch up with you."* If I were more knowledgeable about life or God's Word, I would've added to that comment, "When the lies have caught up with you, what are you going to do? Are you going to confess the truth and be free of bondage or live with the lie for the rest of your life in bondage?"

Food for thought

> *Resolve to be thyself and know that he who finds himself loses his misery. (Matthew Arnold)*

> *Never apologize for having high standards. People who really want to be in your life will rise up to meet them. (Ziad K. Abdelnour)*

> *Many are claiming a new level they'll never reach, because they dishonored the person that was assigned to get them there. When you don't understand the value of relationships and the necessity of honor, you stay stuck in claiming but never obtaining. (Pastor YPJ)*

Growing Up Without God's Guidance

After two and a half years at NCCU, I came home and attended Central Piedmont Community College in Charlotte, North Carolina, to study being a paralegal. After a year there, I changed my major to accounting. There is where I met my son's father (Nathaniel "Spanky" Baker), and I learned that he had attended NCCU also. He was a year behind me. We dated for almost two years. He lived in Monroe, North Carolina, and I was living in Mount Holly, North Carolina, with my mother and two other sisters.

Every weekend, he would come and pick me up to spend the weekend with his family. Of course, that didn't sit well with my mother. So one weekend, he decided to come up early Sunday morning and pick me and my mother up to attend church and have dinner with the family. My mother thought that Langford Chapel Christian Methodist (CME) Church had the most hospitable ushers she'd ever met in her life. It still didn't matter how nice his family was to us or how hospitable the ushers were; she just didn't like my going down that often. I discontinued going every weekend and only went on special occasions.

After dating for two years, our relationship status changed. We had a child on the way. Well, I was afraid to tell my mother. I remember that she told us, "Whenever you make your bed, you have to lie in it." In simple words, "Whatever choices you make in life, you have to live with them." After telling our parents, we decided to get married. I wanted to stay with my mother and be in the home I was raised in. That didn't go over well at all. Spanky said it doesn't work that way, and both sets of parents agreed. *Well, shut the front door!* I was indeed scared of not being with my own mother and not being in the house where I grew up. I was well taken care of by my new family. Our son's grandmother on his father's side was named Zada Baker, and his grandfather was Sam Baker. Our son's great-grandmother, Nancy McKenzie, was alive, and she was in her nineties.

I have no complaints about living with my in-laws until we were financially able to get our own place. I must say he idolized his papa (Sam Baker), who was very protective of him.

Wow, his great-grandmother helped with caring for Butch. She was very alert. When I say that I didn't have God's guidance, it's because I didn't know God in that manner. He was with me all the time, and I didn't have any idea. Having his great-grandmother alive when he was born was a blessing. She saved his life when he broke a piece of plastic that was attached to the side of his bed. This mobile toy would slowly turn. Butch reached up, tore a piece of it, and put it in his mouth. He was about three months old. We had no idea he had torn it until he started gagging and coughing, and we started tapping him in the back, and I put my hand in his mouth when I noticed the broken piece off the mobile. He stopped coughing for a few seconds, and then he started coughing again. His great-grandmother grabbed him, put him on his side on her lap, stuck her finger at the back of his throat, and pulled that piece of plastic out. YES! YES! That toy was a gift and was immediately trashed. We never purchased or received any more gifts made of that flimsy plastic.

I was very protective of his surroundings, especially when it came to babysitting him. I learned from my mama the importance of knowing who your child is around every day because it can affect how they will live their lives and what they find to be most important in life. I must say I did my best. I said I didn't have God's guidance growing up with my only child, but I did. I had my in-laws and my mom.

My mom never talked ugly to me when I was pregnant with my son and when we decided to raise him as a family with both parents. I am so grateful for my son and all the things in life he has accomplished. I wouldn't have it any other way.

WHO ARE THE CHRISTIANS IN THE CHURCH?

As mothers, grandmothers, and great-grandmothers, we all want the best for our children, regardless of their ages. Many of us have probably prayed for them all of our lives and have recited *Proverbs 22:6 (NIV), "Train a child in the way he should go, and when he is old he will not turn from it."* After reading Matthew Henry's commentary about that scripture, it stated that it wasn't written as a promise that your child wouldn't stray. I know that I had a praying mother because I strayed from God's Word and her teaching. But God was with me because I am still here and studying His Word for my own understanding.

I can't change my past, and I definitely don't waste my time and crowd my brain with *what-ifs*. I don't beat myself up over my past. I can truly say that I learned from my past. I praise God for allowing me to turn my life around. I don't boast about my past, but I just acknowledge that I wasn't and I'm not perfect now, but I do know how to ask for forgiveness, knowing that God knows my heart. God doesn't require that I have such a fancy prayer but that, when asking for forgiveness, I pray with faith and passion.

I am so glad that I came up during the era when the Elders took to heart the African proverb that states, *"It takes a village to raise a child."* It seems so different now than when I was a child. To me, it seems that this younger generation prefers to throw that proverb out the window. It's JUST MY THOUGHTS and observations of some young families. My son often reminds me that this is a different generation. FOR SHO! You best not put your hand on someone's child or even try to correct them without upsetting a parent.

When I think about growing up without *following* God's guidance, I know that *2 Timothy 3:1–5 speaks of godlessness in the last days. In the second verse of that scripture, it mentions the disobedience of children to their parents.* We must keep praying for our children and *one another*. Prayer does change things and people. I am a firm believer that Satan is a firm believer in prayer, not because he practices it but because he suffers from it. So let's bombard heaven with prayers.

This is a time when we really need to understand the African proverb and work harder at becoming that village—a village that will set a correct and godly atmosphere for our youth because they are watching us.

Introduced to the Christian Methodist Episcopal Church (CME) with a Baptist Background

In 1967, at the age of twenty-one, I married Nathaniel "Spanky" Baker and moved to Monroe, North Carolina. There, I joined Langford Chapel CME Church, where he attended. I learned that the church was governed by many rules in a book known as *The Book of Discipline of the Christian Methodist Episcopal (CME) Church.* This book explained the basic principles of the Christian Methodist Episcopal Church's organizational structure.

I had no idea that a church had to be governed by rules other than the Bible. I thought, *What have I gotten myself into? Is this some form of cult?* I knew nothing about the structure of the CME. Their structure was new to me because my grandfather, Ferdinand Gibson, was a Baptist pastor in Mount Holly, North Carolina, my hometown. (I stated in another chapter that I wasn't able to attend services that my mother attended because there wasn't enough room in the car for the children.)

I attended Mount Sinai Baptist Church, which was within walking distance from our home. At a young age, I wasn't aware that being part of a youth group known as Baptist Training Union (BTU) was considered part of a structure. I thought that was a name given because we were young and were taught different lessons, such as how to carry ourselves in a godly manner. We would do skits about how to be nice to one another and learn the meaning of the scriptures. These meetings occur yearly with youths from other Baptist churches in Charlotte, Gastonia, and other nearby areas. I thought of it like a vacation Bible school.

As a child, I do remember some Baptist activities that I didn't understand, such as the following:

1. My uncle, Doyle Gibson, would come by the house and collect money when my mother and some of the other members in the area weren't able to come to church. Sometimes he would come by on Saturdays to get the offerings and sometimes on Sunday mornings before Sunday school. He did this until he earned his wings.
2. I remember once a month, a group of women (from my grandfather's church) would meet at different members' homes, and they would sing a hymn, pray, read a scripture, and discuss the Bible and activities that needed to take place at church. When they came to our house, all the children had to go outside. I guess my mom didn't want us hanging around like hungry hound dogs because food was provided and there were rarely any leftovers. This group was called a circle, and they were identified by a number because there were different groups from the same church that gathered in other homes. They were grouped together based on where they lived. I thought they did that just as a way of studying and doing God's work. I later learned in my adult life that that was part of the structure of the Baptist church. As a matter of fact, I remember that my son's great-grandmother, Mrs. Nancy McKenzie, was part of a similar organization in the CME church, and they were called Stewardesses. They met at the church.

As a youth, I recall during church services at Mount Sinai Baptist Church, where I attended until I went off to college at North Carolina Central University in Durham, North Carolina, how members would start crying and hollering loudly when Mr. Henderson or

Mr. Bubba would pray (that wasn't his real name, but it's what he was called). Sometimes, some people would stand up and start singing while they were praying. The ushers would go to those who were hollering and start fanning them. My thought was that they were trying to calm them down so the prayer could be heard.

My cousins and I would look at each other and laugh at the Elders who were hollering. But that didn't last long because we would get a funny look from the ushers or another adult. It still didn't stop us. It got to the point where we would say the prayer with them because we memorized the prayer they would say because they prayed the same prayer. We were told by the ushers that they were going to tell our parents. In a low voice, we still recited their prayers with them. In our defense, we said we would ask our parents, "Isn't it good to learn how to pray?" (LOL) So as a Baptist member, I really never thought there was such a thing as organizational structure.

So when I got married at twenty-one and started attending a CME Church, I was lost about church structures, and even then, at that age, I was married and had a child on the way. I still wasn't interested in the rules or the *Discipline* book by which they were governed. It wasn't a question in my mind as to whether I was going to church. I knew better. I was happy just being part of the choir.

After my son, Robert "Butch" LaVelle Baker, was born and when he turned three or four, I started teaching children Sunday school. I taught Sunday school and sang in the choir for years. Still, I never attended any of the Langford Chapel church conferences. (That's when they discussed church business.) I never picked up or owned a *Discipline*. I said I didn't need all that to be a Christian or a member. It was a lot to read, and I still wasn't interested. I was young and had no interest in anything but taking care of my son and going to work.

My father-in-law, Samuel Baker, at that time, would attend meetings he called district meetings and sometimes annual conferences. When my son's father, Nathaniel "Spanky" Baker, would work on Saturdays and there was a meeting out of town, my father-in-law would ask if my son and I wanted to go with him. So we would travel with him, and my son and I would follow him around and make sure he didn't get out of our sight.

I didn't have any idea what was being said or the importance of what was being said. He was a very smart and kind man. During breaks, he would try to explain what went on in the meeting and why they had to meet separately from the other groups. He said we were in the lay meeting. *What are lay people, and what do they have to do with the church?* Trying to explain that information to me was like pouring water on a duck's back. I DIDN'T CARE! I still thought the Bible was the main book to have in a church. I did enjoy the trip. Remember, I was young and still naive. All I knew was that we went to church on Sundays and had choir rehearsals on Thursdays.

I remember after attending Langford Chapel for a few years with still no "*Discipline* knowledge," the church hosted what was known as the Durham District Conference. Well, I thought it was like a big church reunion, and these different churches were all invited. The church had to set up different rooms and locations for the people to meet. (It reminded me of when I was a Baptist member, and once a year, we would have a gathering like that. I never thought of it as having the same structure.)

So after devotion, they were assigning the groups (organizations) to rooms. Several had to meet in the church sanctuary because of the limited space. I heard my father-in-law calling, "Lulu [that was a nickname he and my mother-in-law, Mrs. Zada Baker, had given me], go to the lay meeting."

"Okay," I said, but under my breath, I asked myself, *Who are they, and what do they do or represent?* That question was running through my mind as I followed a group headed to the rear of the church. I was active in church as the children's Sunday school teacher and a member of the choir, but I wasn't familiar with the *Discipline*.

A funny thing happened during the district conference. I was elected secretary for the lay organization for the Durham District. One thing in my favor was that I knew what a secretary did. My son and I attended several meetings with his grandfather, but I still didn't have any clue or comprehension of what I was to do or what was expected of me. I knew the church talked about the *Discipline*, but I never picked it up for understanding.

Notes from the lay organization were distributed during the conference about the structure of the organization. I still wasn't ready or qualified for the secretary position because of a lack of knowledge of the organization. I should not have been elected. The young lady who was my opponent is now a minister. She was also known throughout the conference. She should've been elected. I wasn't known at the conference.

I feel that my father-in-law's being well-known played a great part in my being elected, as did the conference being held at our church. She was chosen as assistant secretary because no one else offered themselves for that position. I am saying this now because, sadly, it still exists, not just in the local churches but throughout the CME conferences. People are placed in positions because of who they are or because they are well known or liked. NOTED!

I thought that it was all about me and a bag of chips when I was elected as secretary. I was young and ignorant of the purpose of the organization to which I was elected. Well, the chip bag was empty. I had no idea what format to use to type the minutes. I definitely had to have help typing it fast enough to present it to the rest of the conference after each group met and reassembled. The typewriter was very old, and you had to hit the keys hard. It was like the old Royal typewriters. (You, young people, google and see what the typewriter looked like.)

Well, my bubble burst because I needed help. Just that quickly, the position didn't seem important. Then I was told a couple of months later that I would need to send those minutes to someone else who was over all the districts. *All* the districts? The only district I knew of was the District of Columbia. Yes, I'm talking about Washington, District of Columbia—DC. I knew that district because we visited family there. Well, to make a long story short, I told my father-in-law that I couldn't continue being the secretary because it was interfering with my time with my son. My excuse! He told me to do what I felt was best for me and my son. I chose to resign.

WHO ARE THE CHRISTIANS IN THE CHURCH?

I never participated in any district or church organization that involved my knowing the *Discipline*. I just wanted to be in the choir and teach the young children of the church. (Teaching is one of my gifts from God, and it was easy working with the very young children. I did use the CME to publish books for very young children.) As I said earlier, I should've never been elected, nor should I have accepted the position. What occurred then was WRONG!

Those actions brought to mind the *Negro Politics*[1]. Negro politics, as James Q. Wilson described it, was a device that was used to justify self and to bring accolades to the individual presiding. To some people, it wasn't necessarily wrong, but when you aren't in keeping with God's Word and God's laws, then it's wrong. I have seen so much of it in the church, and we have become so numb to it—numb to the fact that it has almost destroyed our churches. We have to wake up and be accountable to God for what we do, and God will direct our path. We must acknowledge that with authority comes the need for accountability. With prosperity comes the need for integrity. Having integrity will help guard our hearts against greed. Our path is undirected because of how we are doing things in God's house.

We're no worse or no better than the money changers who were in the temple, and Jesus became angry because the buyers were being cheated, which in itself was wrong, but the sellers were disrespecting the temple, which was set aside for worshippers to be in the presence of God. We don't call the place where we assemble to worship God the temple. We are the temple.

We have to be careful how we are doing things and why we are doing them. We are not doing things to justify or please others, but only to please God. Yes, we have a director over what we are doing, and yes, we are supposed to be able to go to that director to discuss our issues, but some of us are afraid of our position because retribution can take place. We are afraid that once we get too close to the

---

[1] James Q. Wilson, *Negro Politics: The Search for Leadership*. James has a PhD in political science. His dissertation was an analysis of the political behavior of African Americans in Chicago in the 1950s and was the basis for his first book, *Negro Politics: The Search for Leadership* (1960).

mirror, we often fall in line with what has transpired and taken place, and that in itself is hurting the growth of our churches. Our churches should be based on love and consideration for one another and not on how high or how far we can climb to the top, regardless of whom we step on or hurt in the process.

Yes, we have aspirations to move, but it should not be in the process of destroying someone else to reach a higher level. While studying and reading *Negro Politics*, I remember it speaking of the negro leaders who were educated, members of a fraternity, civic leaders, held a high position in the church, members of the NAACP, and possibly members of the YMCA. I would also like to add to the list someone who served in the military in a high position. The book spoke of the men as those who weren't interested in reaching back to help their fellow man but were only concerned with how they looked in the eyes of society. As their "phraseology," they were "ditty, high sedity, or silk stocking"—a person who dresses richly and luxuriously. This image was more important than caring, loving, and helping one another.

Romans 12:3 says,

> *For by the grace [of God] given to me I say to every one of you not to think more highly of himself [and of his importance and ability] than he ought to think; but to think so as to have sound judgment, as God has apportioned to each a degree of faith [and a purpose designed for service]. (AMP)*

Life-Changing Moment
Leaving Monroe After Almost Ten Years

I WAS A MEMBER of Langford Chapel for almost ten years. During the early summer of 1976, my son and I moved to Charlotte, North Carolina. His father and I thought we were better friends than spouses. We weren't angry; we just saw life through a different lens. During that era (1967) and up to the time before I left Monroe (1977), women couldn't get cars or own things in their names; they had to get their spouse's or a male's name on the purchase of cars or mortgages. Well, I purchased a car, and it was in my spouse's name. Of course, it wasn't brand-new, but I didn't have any problems with it. A gentleman who was renting a room at my in-laws' house worked at the dealership, and he made sure the car was in good condition.

My husband, our son Robert LaVelle "Butch" Baker, and I were going to rent a house about four miles from Monroe, which was near Wingate College. I don't know why my husband decided to drive my car to check on the house. On the way home, an intoxicated woman came over the hill on the wrong side of the road and hit him head-on. They found drugs in her car. Needless to say, my car was totaled. Yes, I was SOL. I technically didn't own a car anymore. My son's father had a nice Buick Riviera, but he didn't drive it to work because his mother said people would think that you, being young and Black, didn't need that job. So he drove an older Chrysler she owned and let her drive the Riviera through the week, and he drove his car on the weekend, or if he wanted to go out somewhere other than work, he would drive his car.

After about two weeks, I was concerned as to why I hadn't received the check for my car. When I checked with the insurance company, they informed me that the check was mailed a week ago to my ex, and they told me how much it was. When I asked my ex where the check for my car was, he told me he loaned it to his brother so he could get a car. KNOW THIS! I didn't have a bridle over my tongue when I made it clear that at the end of the next week (which was his payday), I wanted the exact amount of the check because I needed a car. I had started working as an inspector in a cloth factory. My sister-in-law also worked there, so I rode to work with her. If I needed transportation to go anywhere other than work, I would call my father-in-law to take me.

The Sunday following the accident, Butch and I had to catch a ride to church. When we arrived home after church services, Butch had a temperature of 101 degrees. I called his grandfather and asked if he could take us to the ER because of Butch's fever. He asked where his son was. I told him he had decided he was going to Cheraw, South Carolina, to hang out with some of his workers (who were a mother and her three daughters; they all worked at the same factory). TRUST ME. There wasn't any drama going on there (LOL).

After returning home from the ER, he told me to tell his son to come see him. Of course, he got a butt chewing from his father, and he came home and was going to make it sound like I threw him under the bus because his father was very upset. Yes, he was upset because he chose not to go to church instead of going to Cheraw, South Carolina. The worst part of this situation was the many sickening excuses he gave for going to Cheraw, South Carolina, and not church. But he made a bad move when he tried to intimidate me by saying ungodly things to me at close range.

When I had enough of the noise—and he was upsetting my child—I turned around with an open fist and slapped him so hard that the left side of his face instantly swelled, and my fingerprints were easily showing on his face. All he could do was cry and apologize. Neither affected me, nor did I care. That was the first time he had ever tried me. He was hurt by the fact that his father was disappointed, not that he wasn't available to take his son to the ER.

I never told his father how he would leave on Fridays after work and come home on Sunday night, lighting up the house and smelling like marijuana. He found out on his own. My son never heard me say anything negative about his father. I always wanted to learn about people through my own observation, and I wanted Butch to learn about people the way he sees them and not from the opinion of someone else.

The following weekend, I did get the cash for my car. I went to the same dealership and got a brand-new car in my ex's name. Before the next car payment was due, I informed him, after informing his father, that Butch and I were moving to Charlotte. He didn't seem surprised or as if it even mattered. I guess under his breath, he probably said, "No more lies on Fridays that I'm going to the store to get a pack of cigarettes or going to the ABC store."

He asked when that decision about moving was made. My response was, "I thought it was time for us to live our different lives apart. I didn't want our son to live in a home where the parents' lives were totally different. It's not fair for him to be lied to every weekend because you leave for two days and are not home to play games with him like I do. So it wasn't a hard decision to make." I told Butch we would be moving because I needed to move closer to my job.

I had been working at the Charlotte Housing Authority for almost a year. When Lorraine, the manager in Monroe, started working in Charlotte, she asked me to come and work at one of the housing projects that needed an assistant manager, so I took the job. I told Butch he could still come and visit his papa and big mama (his grandmother in Monroe). He was cool with that. After telling Spanky (his father) and Mr. Baker of my plans to move, I went to my son's grandparents' home and overheard his sister telling her mother about my move, but there were some incorrect comments made. I walked into the room and said, "Let me tell you that the correct reason we are moving is that your son failed to tell you the truth."

When we moved, I didn't have to purchase any furniture. I took the furniture with me. A couple of the fellows who worked with me drove the U-Haul truck and moved Butch and me.

One of his family members told him to file for custody of our son. I would rather leave the person who suggested filing for custody out of the picture, or, should I say, out of my life story. I reminded him, "*That might just be the nail in your coffin. Go ahead!*" I didn't want him or anyone else to feel that they owed me anything. I would love to hear him tell the judge why he would be a better parent than me to raise our son. "Oh, I make more money and have a better car, and when I want to just hang out all weekend, I could have my dad pick him up from school, and I would see him Sunday evening when I come home." I don't think either the judge or his grandparents would go along with that.

I was raised to be independent, and indeed, I didn't waver from it. Spanky, the nickname for Butch's father, had very cloudy lenses when it came to not being able to see that his father was the "father figure" in our son's life. I gave him what he thought would help him with his identity crisis, but that wasn't the only issue he had. Apparently, having a child wasn't the cure.

We've heard the old saying that one is known by the company they keep. My ex-husband's friends were those whom many older Christians called ill repute. My son's grandfather was very sad when I told him that my son, Butch, and I were moving to Charlotte to be closer to my family. As you can see, I have often mentioned how we (Mr. Baker and I) respected each other and what a great role model he was for my son. I never talked negatively to my son about his father. He was only a child, and he knew that his father wasn't in the picture for most of his younger years, so the move wasn't upsetting to him.

The day that I moved to Charlotte, I dropped off the new car, the one in my ex's name, at the dealership where I purchased a car in *my* name. Several days later, I received a call to come and move my car. I told him the owner of that car lives in Monroe, and I gave them the number to contact him. I never received another call.

A funny thing happened after we moved to Charlotte. I went to Monroe to pick up my son on a Saturday, and the house phone rang. I was asked to answer the phone because I was closest to it since I was coming out of the bathroom. His grandparents and great-grandmother were the only ones home, and they were sitting on the front porch. It so happened to be the car dealership calling for Butch's father. I stated that he wasn't there, and they wanted to know if I had his address. I said, "You've got the correct address and phone number." Well, the dealer picked the car up in Charlotte, and he had to make the monthly payment and the storage charge while the car was in Charlotte at the dealer where I bought a car in my name. I told his family that someone was looking for Spanky. If I were a betting person, I'm sure his father spent very little time with him because I had to go get him. What's new? SOS.

When my family learned that I had moved to Charlotte, they were surprised and upset that I hadn't told them. My mother never involved herself in any of her children's homes, nor did she ask questions as to what was going on with them. But she was surprised that I never gave any hint that there was a problem in my marriage. I told them all that I didn't want them to form any opinions about my ex or my family. I reminded them that we were taught well.

We were told that if we make our own "bed," we have to lie in it. The *bed* in that comment is a metaphor. This simply means that we have to make the most of the life we choose or work it out. I told them I chose to get out. One sister was adamant about not letting him go or spend time with his father. I said, "I am not upset about the move, nor am I angry. I am not using my child as a pawn to get back at his father." The Lord knows I definitely need a break as well. Even just to piddle around in the house.

I never tried or wanted to interfere with him wanting to see our son or taking him to Monroe for a weekend visit. I knew he wouldn't try anything contrary to the court orders. You see, I had already made contact with an attorney, and he had all the facts he needed, and my ex didn't want his lifestyle brought up in court.

The duplex we moved into was in a quiet neighborhood in Charlotte. He immediately met two brothers, Eric and Greg, and one of their cousins, Brian, who lived on the same street as us. They attended the same elementary and middle schools. They also played basketball for Plaza United Methodist Church, which was located in the neighborhood. They were very welcome to play with them, and he met more new friends. I kept him involved in sports and the Cub Scouts.

My first fear of him not being with a family member was when he decided to go camping with the Cub Scouts. I told his leader that he hasn't ever gone anywhere without the presence of a family member and that I'm not sure if he will want to go since we are new to Charlotte. Well, he decided he wanted to go. I thought, *Oh, Lord! What am I going to say to discourage him from going?* I was so afraid that something might happen to him.

I have never experienced his absence except when he went out of town with his grandparents when we lived in Monroe. I didn't want my child out of my sight except when he went to Monroe to be with his father and his family. It was an overnight trip, but it was still too much for me to handle. I could hardly sleep that night. I was expecting a call from the Cub leader saying that he wanted to come home, but there was no call! When I got a call, it was the next day, and it was to tell me they were back and that I could pick Butch up at the church. It was the same church where he played basketball. He said he had a good time. Boy! I was glad and sad to hear that. I wanted him to miss me. That didn't happen.

I learned that my son was a leader, and the Cub Scout leader told me what a big help he was when they had "chats" around the campfire. I thought coming from a one-parent home now would cause him to be shy or embarrassed, but it didn't faze him. My son loved his grandfather, Sam Baker, so much that it didn't seem like he was from a one-parent home because he would call and check on him as well as his father. My father was into construction and was rarely around enough for my son to really get to know him, and my parents lived in Mount Holly, North Carolina, about fifty miles from Monroe and about fifteen miles from Charlotte. When Butch and I visited my mom, my father wasn't around. He worked in New York and the DC area.

Another easy element of the move was the fact that I had been working in Charlotte for over a year at Earle Village Charlotte Housing Authority. This is where I found help to move to Charlotte. Butch was very comfortable going to a new school and meeting new friends. The after-school daycare was very secure, and he made new friends there as well. On several days while working at Earle Village Housing, I had the opportunity to take Butch to work with me, especially when he had doctor's appointments. Thank God, he has never had a problem meeting people. I had to do a home visit at an apartment, which was in the same area where I parked my car. I introduced him to several young boys his age. I knew them and their mother very well, and over forty years later, they are still friends.

Even with the move in 1977, we still didn't miss a beat attending church. I immediately decided to go to one of the three CME churches in Charlotte. I chose to attend Parkwood CME Church because I had met some of the ladies from that church while attending conferences with my former father-in-law. After attending Parkwood CME Church for about six months, I felt that the church was too big for me. I was more familiar with smaller churches than larger ones. Parkwood had about six hundred members, and I felt like I would only be able to sing in the choir or just be a member. All the positions were filled, and I was never asked to participate in or join any church organization. I decided to just attend worship services. I felt I probably could've joined the choir, but I wasn't invited. I didn't get that opportunity. Not knowing the *Book of Discipline*, I wasn't sure if there was some form of protocol to be part of the choir or any organization. Feeling left out or not comfortable just going to church and not being involved in anything, I decided to check out one of the other CME churches closer to where I lived.

I chose to attend Faith CME in Hidden Valley. I eventually moved to a home in that area. The church's history states it was established in 1975 in the Hidden Valley community. Twelve members from Parkwood CME Church had been recruited to start that church. I was told that the pastor who was assigned to that church had not arrived because of his commitment to another position. So the bishop (in layman's terms, the CEO over an assigned episcopacy of churches) recruited members and Elders to walk the streets of Hidden Valley to campaign, invite, and introduce the new church to the neighborhood.

The CME Church had other ministers to fill in until the assigned pastor arrived. From the information I received about the church from one of the recruits from Parkwood, Mrs. Juanita Audrey, it was about two years before the assigned pastor arrived, which was approximately in the early fall of 1977. My son, Robert LaVelle "Butch" Baker, and I started attending Faith CME in January of 1978. The first pastor who had been assigned there had left, but they had someone else, whom they called an Elder, who was the interim pastor.

When I looked around the church, I saw quite a few older people there. As you know by now, I didn't know why he was called Elder Meriwether. Of course, *elder* wasn't his first name but his position in the structure of the CME Church. Okay, I didn't know that. You are correct if you said I still had no knowledge or ownership of the CME *Discipline*. The person preaching was called an Elder because of his status in the church structure. In business, he would be like an area manager. He was there until it was time for the annual conference and a new pastor would be assigned to the church.

The next pastor charged with the church, the late Reverend Robyn Gool, came from Oral Roberts University, located in Oklahoma. His teaching and presence were totally different from what I used to hear. His teaching reminded me of preachers I heard on television. Well, he drew many members to join the church. We almost outgrew the church. You had to get there early to get a seat. There were all members on the balcony.

I don't recall if the CME *Discipline* was ever mentioned or expounded on during Rev. Robyn Gool's tenure or not. What I did know was that he did minister about tithing. He talked about it quite often. I could not digest it because of my intellectual level of tithing to God. My focus was on raising my son and living on my salary. To me, it sounded like a cult. Yes, I had my Bible and my highlighter, but I didn't read for my own knowledge.

To be honest, after hearing it so much, it really turned me off. I gave what I thought I could afford. (Ouch! It hurts to say this now, but the truth must be told.) I had not joined Faith CME, so I figured it was for the members and not for me to tithe. I would come up

WHO ARE THE CHRISTIANS IN THE CHURCH?

with excuses to be exempted from tithing. It sounds so stupid saying it now because I know better, but I had to think of surviving during that era of my life. I was just attending church for the first year that Rev. Robyn Gool became the pastor of Faith CME Church. Paying what I could or what I just thought was good enough was okay with me. I didn't feel as if I was cheating God. I really felt I had to do the best I could and prayed that God understood my situation. I wasn't sure if God really wanted me to do that based on my salary, and He knew my son's father had gone as many as six months without paying child support. I still wasn't fully committed to tithing even after being asked how I could expect God to bless me when I wasn't doing what He required of me as a "Christian." I still hadn't gotten to that level of knowing God as my Lord, Savior, and provider.

I will never forget when Rev. Gool had been at Faith CME for almost two years. He announced to the television crew on site that he was led by God to start a church with his spouse. How did they know? It was a big shocker to most of the members. Some had already planned to leave with him. Over half of the church left. I was approached to see if I was leaving because his wife and I were very close. I said no. I joined Faith CME, not the pastor.

Well, there I was at my second church in Charlotte, North Carolina, and the second pastor was leaving. I enjoyed the members, so I had no intention of leaving the church. The one thing I knew for sure was that, at the upcoming annual conference, a new pastor would be assigned. The odd thing about that was that you never knew who was going to be your next pastor until Saturday, near the closing of the conference, or the following Sunday, when they appeared in the pulpit.

I still call myself a CME, even after the changing of the pastors. I must say I still didn't know what to expect or whether I had made the right move by changing churches. "We will see," I kept telling myself. It turned out to be a great choice. The members seemed very close and loving toward one another—like a big family.

I knew that I had to continue attending church, and I made sure it was instilled in my son's life. Until he turned eighteen, I had a great support group, mostly from the Faith CME family, and a family friend who wanted to make sure he had a male figure in his face if the need should arise. The father of his best friend Ed Mason, the late Ed Mason, said he was going to take him under his wing because he wanted to make sure I didn't make a "softie" out of him. Yes, he meant he wanted to make sure he was tough. I made it known that I don't teach my son to fight. He said that's why he would keep an eye on him.

Moving to Charlotte was a bold move for me. I didn't visit Charlotte regularly when I lived in Mount Holly, North Carolina. I am not the best person to deal well with change. So I had many thoughts going through my mind about my decision to move. But I knew I was getting out of the living situation I was in. That was never a second thought.

Charlotte was so big for me, and all I could think about was the high crime rate here. Well, we survived our new home and new church. In my early thirties, that was my main concern. Yes, my priorities were out of order, but I was in survival mode and had a lack of knowledge of God's Word. I was putting my opinion first and what I thought was important, and I felt God knew my heart.

I must say that after Butch's graduation from high school and the military, it was a different story. He was grown-up. He met his present wife, Monica Hinton Baker, while in the navy in Norfolk, Virginia. I thank God for their thirty-three-year marriage with six children and five grandchildren. I just learned another great-granddaughter will be arriving in late spring.

As mothers, grandmothers, and great-grandmothers, we all want the best for our children, regardless of their ages. Many of us have probably prayed for them all of our lives and have recited Proverbs 22:6, "Train a child in the way he should go, and when he is old he will not turn from it" (NIV). I know that I had a praying mother because I strayed from God's Word and her teaching. But God is still with me because I am still here and studying His Word for my own understanding.

Welcome Reverend Anthony L. Williams and Family

Welcome Rev. Anthony L. Williams, Lady Laverne, and daughter Charity to Faith CME Church. Near the closing of the annual conference, pastors receive their church assignment, or, as we say, their "charge." These charges are assigned yearly. Usually, the delegates from the various churches will contact some of the members of the church with information as to whether the former pastor will return or if there will be a new pastor arriving.

In most cases, if a pastor had a new assignment, they would meet with the delegates from their new charge and request to meet certain officers and other members later that day. This is how they get a chance to meet the officers in charge of the finances in our churches, who are called stewards, and the trustees, who are responsible for the property, and the stewardess, known usually in conjunction with the stewards to make appropriations for the pastor. The funny thing about a new pastor in town is that they can draw members who may have been lost from sight; in other words, they hadn't been coming to church, but they would make that meeting.

If you are wondering how they got the word, they would contact another member to see if a new pastor was assigned. If the stewards and stewardess receive word that there will be a new pastor arriving, they are responsible for making hotel accommodations and, of course, preparing snacks like fruit, water, and other beverages available. If they are new to the area, they will show them where they will be staying and the best route to the church. (This is before MapQuest.) I was there because I was the new assistant superintendent of Sunday school. I even joined the choir. I was no longer just a "bench sitter."

After introducing himself and his family at the meeting, our new pastor shared his expectations. He spoke of those expectations with a soft voice. Some of his expectations were shockers for some of us. The very first statement he made was, *"Do not schedule or accept any invitations on Friday nights because that is a family fight with my family."* He was very adamant about it. It was received as under no situation will he be available, except for an emergency. Whoa! It was easily understood. *He also added that there should not and must not be any meetings after church services.* He explained the importance of how all families should spend quality time together. Well taken. He knew that a lot of evangelism had taken place in the neighborhood before having an assigned pastor there. Second, he firmly stated that *no one would be part of the evangelism team unless they completed an evangelism class,* which would meet for one hour weekly for approximately six weeks. At a later date, he would ask who would like to be on the team so books could be ordered. He told us to be assured that the Jehovah's Witnesses have to complete classes and training before knocking on doors. I thought, *Each pastor must have their own agenda.*

We all quietly listened to what he had to say. (The floor wasn't opened for any questions or comments at that point.) For the third comment, he said, *"It is very important that if you are an officer in the church, you* must *and are required to have ownership of a Discipline."* Well, let me slide under a pew! At that moment, I didn't know whether to say *ouch* or to just keep a straight face and not make a guilty grunt or any sound, and I definitely didn't want to make eye contact with him because my eyes would've had a *say-what?* look. He made it plain that the *Discipline* is the official expression of our faith, the way our church is governed, and our spiritual and legal guide.

The next expectation he said was that all officers must bring their *Discipline* to the next scheduled church conference. For those of us who probably had a "why bring it to the church conference meeting" look on our faces, he commented, "In case you have a question about anything I said or any actions I requested, then we can go to a certain section in the *Discipline*, and the answers would be there." *Well, whoopee ding ding!* I didn't know where or how fast I would have access to the book.

This is when the old saying, "Don't put off tomorrow what you can do today," really comes into play. I had been a CME for almost fourteen years and didn't think I needed a *Discipline*. I wasn't in any important position in the church, and I was in denial, asking myself what the reason was for my purchasing one. Little did I know that just being a member was a good reason. He didn't embarrass anyone by asking who had one. He said that *if* you needed one, give your name to the steward board, and they would order them at once, and we could write a check or give the steward the money when the books arrived.

I must say that Rev. Anthony L. Williams was the first Christian Methodist Episcopal (CME) pastor at Faith CME who enforced having a *Discipline* and the importance of knowing who we are and what we believe. I bought my first *Discipline* under him. I really enjoyed his sermons and his leadership. This was the time I wished bishops didn't move ministers from church to church. I really became attached to him and his family. I learned a lot about our church's history and structure.

Under his leadership, he made it interesting to learn the *Discipline* and the Scriptures. I also got baptized under him after hearing a sermon he preached about putting new wine into an old wineskin. That caught my attention because I wanted to see what in the world a wineskin was and what it had to do with being saved and being a Christian. As you know by now, I stated that, as a child, I was a "why person." I still am a "why person." He spoke from Ephesians 4:22:

> *You were taught, with regard to your former way of life, to put off your old self, which is being corrupt by its deceitful desires; to be made new in the attitude of your minds; and to put on the new self, created to be like God in true righteousness and holiness.*

He gave the following two scriptures referring to the same message: Colossians 3:9–10 and 2 Corinthians 5:17. During that era, we carried our Bibles to church with a yellow highlighter and would write notes in our Bibles. Oh, yeah! I was all but sitting on the edge of my seat, listening to know what this sermon was going to be about. I sat near the front because I didn't want to hear others' conversations during his preaching. Before he came, I sat on or around the six pews, and when I started enjoying how well he explained what he was saying, I moved closer and sat on the third pew. I started bringing a small tablet that would fit inside my Bible bag to take notes of the educational and very informative sermons.

I was extremely close to his wife. It was a joke; sometimes members of the church start calling me Laverne, the name of the pastor's wife. We would joke about how they had kicked me to the curb for her and had forgotten my name (LOL). It was fun knowing that we could joke and laugh with the pastor and his wife. She made it known that she was going to clubs when he met her, and he told her, "I'm going to marry you," and she said, "No, you aren't." (I can relate to that.) She was so approachable and never wanted anyone to feel that she was better than them.

As I write this chapter about someone very special to me, I must say, "Rest in peace, Rev. Anthony L. Williams." After pastoring at Faith CME for several years, he was transferred to the New York/Washington Conference, where he was assigned to a church in Washington, DC. After pastoring there for a few years, he left the Christian Methodist Episcopal Church. He and his wife, Laverne, started their own church, Blessed Assurance Nondenominational, after returning to Charlotte, North Carolina. It was where she started pastoring.

I've learned that people will forget what you say and what you do, but they will never forget how you make them feel.

Thanks for opening my eyes and heart to understanding the journey I must travel to do God's will for my life.

Never Say Never in God's House

I REMEMBER WHEN I was in my early forties I made the comment that there were three positions in the church that I never wanted to serve: being a stewardess, an usher, or a youth Sunday school teacher, especially the youth teacher. I served as superintendent of Sunday school, but I made it known loud and clear (I thought) that I didn't want to deal with other members' youths. Well, lo and behold, God proved me wrong, or He showed me whose I was. Be honest. Have you ever said something crazy like that, or am I the only one God proved different?

Well, I can say that I am laughing now, but when I said in a loud "not going to happen" voice, I lost that fight. My arms and my mouth were too short to box or fight with God. God showed me who was in charge. The pastor, Rev. Willie Sturgess, announced one Sunday after Sunday school that we needed a youth teacher. Well, I looked around to see who was taking on the challenge and wondered why the youth was saying, "Oh, no! Not Mrs. Lorraine." I was looking at them like they were crazy, and the pastor said, "Thanks, Mrs. Lorraine, for volunteering," and the whole time my arm was raised. "No!" I shouted, "I didn't volunteer!" That was the result of my saying what I wasn't going to do in God's house.

I told the pastor that I didn't raise my hand. He laughed and said, "You may not have, but it was up, and the youth said yes that it was raised." After going back and forth with the pastor and with the youths laughing, I realized that God doesn't always play fair.

After church, I tried to plead my case by saying that even the youths didn't want me. But he thought it was funny. I looked at him and said, "Really, are you playing a joke on me?" Still laughing, he told me to read *Hebrews 12:1 (NIV).*

> *Therefore, since we are surrounded by such a great cloud of witnesses, let us throw off everything that hinders and the sin that so easily entangles, and let us run with perseverance the race marked out for us."*

I read it and told him, "I think you are making a big mistake because I don't have a lot of patience with other people, especially teenagers." He informed me that he didn't elect me; God did. Doggone! What could I say? Later that day, I called and said, "Okay, I will give it a try," as if I was doing him a favor. This is one of those times I would've said, "Pray for my strength," but oh, no! God doesn't serve that strength on a silver platter. That strength would come from walking through the valley, the storms, and the mountains. So I just got busy thanking God and said, "With You by my side, everything will be alright."

The following Sunday, I shared my lesson plans with the pastor for approval, which were approved. I wasn't using the CME Church Sunday school books. They (the *Discipline* of the CME Connectional churches) were really strict about using their material. My lesson plan was based on current events and the Bible. I dealt with racism, music (mostly the wordings), forgiveness, and other topics that were of interest to the youth while still making sure that what I taught was based on the Bible.

My first lesson dealt with racism. I invited a young Caucasian lady who worked with me, who moved to Carolina and was married to a Black young man who was from Charlotte. She was excited about talking to the class about her life here in the South being married to a Black man. The class was in awe when she stated that when she first saw him, she saw a handsome and astute gentleman, based on his conversations with others at a gathering in Charlotte. She didn't see just a Black man. They were open and honest about how they felt about mixed marriages. They based their love for each other merely on someone they fell in love with. They knew some people here—in the south, especially—didn't accept their marriage, but their love for each other was solely based on their love and not how society felt. She was from Wisconsin, and they eventually moved there.

When I arrived at work the next day, there was a lovely thank-you card from my coworker, who stated how she really enjoyed the youth. She felt they really expressed themselves so openly, and she felt they understood that it was not about race but about love. For this lesson, I used *Genesis 1:27*: "*So God created man in His own image, in the image of God created He him; male and female created He them.*" The scripture wasn't talking about physical appearance or even ethnicity. He was talking about the mental and spiritual faculties that we share with God. This image distinguishes us from animals. The root of the image is love itself.

I could go on and on about the many topics we discussed, but the main issue for us is to watch what and how we say we aren't going to do what calling God has placed on our lives to do for the upbuilding of His kingdom. I really enjoyed the classes, and most of all, I loved, loved, loved those teenagers and the *tween*agers (those who were younger than thirteen). I encouraged them to always be honest about their feelings because what was said in the class stayed in the class.

No, not one spoke of anything in a manner that was harmful toward themselves or another teen, whether in the class or not. I didn't want any parents to assist me because I felt the students wouldn't feel as comfortable expressing themselves.

The youths were very astute with their learning because of the environment in which they were brought up. They were very open-minded about different aspects of life. I had two youths, Asali and Keisha, who were very open-minded about the topics we discussed. They called a rose a rose. As the old saying goes from the poem of Gertrude Stein, "A rose is a rose is a rose." It means that "things are what they are." They called a rose a rose, and regardless of the color, it still smells the same to them.

In one session, I learned what a *wannabe* was. It's someone who doesn't have the aptitude to become who they think they are. The youth taught me that word. See? We are never too old to learn. LOL.

Well, that's what my book is all about—Christians perpetrating a life that's not suitable for the teaching of God's Word.

Do you know what calling God has for your life? I have been told by several pastors that I am running from my calling to the ministry. I would say, "No, I am called to teach." I need to stay in my lane and not be led by what someone other than God says I should be doing. If I hadn't taught that class of teenagers, I would've missed a blessing in life. Jewel Inspiration had a quote that said, *"Blessings are like glitter; they fall gently around us. You don't always see them until you look from a different perspective."* I definitely saw the youth from a different perspective. We need to be aware that, at the tender age of youth, we also play a role in molding their lives.

We must all find our purpose in life. Regardless of our age, God has a purpose for all of us. Well, since I started writing my book, God said, "By the way, you will be serving on the usher board and the stewardess board." Here I am at seventy-six years old. God showed up to remind me that I have work to do. He didn't slow-walk me down. He knew when it was time, and if I tried to say no, I would remember that God does not play fair, and the fear came upon me.

I said yes to both, and my husband thought it was so funny and said, "I told you so." When I looked back over my life, I asked for God's forgiveness. There could've been an alternative. I laughed and gave God praise for showing favor in my life.

On my first Sunday ushering, I felt like a load had been lifted. A word of advice: "Never say never in God's house." When I think about it, it's a blessing to serve God. Hallelujah!

Mahatma Gandhi, a well-known transformative and inspirational speaker, and fearless campaigner for civil rights, sadly said to Martin Luther King, "I like your Christ, but I don't like your Christians. Your Christians are so unlike your Christ."

The Untamable Tongue

I REMEMBER WHEN THE late Reverend Anthony Williams preached about the danger of the tongue from the entire book of James 3. The title of the sermon really caught my attention. The book of James in the New Testament speaks of how hard it is to tame a human tongue. It talks about how bits are placed in a horse's mouth to control them. As small as the tongue is, it is harder to control than a ship with a rudder. Well, I knew this sermon would keep my full attention because this was one of my worst self-destructions.

When you were very young, how often were you told to "shut up" or "be quiet"? Maybe you can't remember how many times, but you might say, "I do know that I was popped on the lips for some things I would say or wouldn't stop talking when told to." My mother always had words of advice when we were out of order. I can't remember the number of times I was punished, but I do recall the statement she would say to me, "Your mouth is going to be the death of you." Ouch! That sounded so cold to tell a young person. I thought someone was going to kill me for saying what I wanted to say. Have you experienced the "you are just like your father or mother" situation? I was told that I was just like my father. I have to get the last word in. I guess she was correct, or, I should say, surely she knew best.

Well, I must say that as I grew older, my tendency to talk didn't decrease but increased approximately threefold. It became worse in my high school years. I had no problem cutting you down even before God had a chance to correct my thinking. My mouth was like a cartoon character named Quick Draw McGraw. He was a sheriff's horse who wore a six-shooter and would accidentally shoot himself in the foot. Every time it happened, I would laugh hysterically, not knowing I was doing the same to myself with my tongue. I didn't stop saying what I wanted to say until I felt satisfied that I got the best of you, because when I would go off like that, it was because I was attacked first, so I felt that the end of the attack belonged to me. Yes! I took advantage of it, and I never felt any remorse about what I said.

While writing this book, it hit me hard in the chest, but it's best to tell the truth because I have to say there were repercussions later in life from the way I handled my reactions. I need to share how it eventually caught up with me and how I learned that I was not doing the will of God for my life.

After high school, I studied sociology as my major. During my study of people, I learned what triggers irate emotions, such as going off brutally on someone. In my early years, I became disappointed with someone close to me, and I never felt comfortable sharing with anyone. I didn't have much or very little trust in people except my mother, and I was embarrassed to talk to her about how I felt. She always knew something was going on, and I would blame it on being so busy and tired. I allowed it to linger around for years, and it just festered and caused me to become agitated.

One job I really enjoyed had to come to an end after working there for about fourteen years. I had a lot of freedom on the job, but I was ready for a change to move up to a different scale. My manager supported me in the job I was doing and was elated that I learned most of it from reading a DOT (Department of Transportation) book on my own. I was working in the safety department of a well-known trucking company. Of course, you know the drill: You teach someone from outside the company how to do what you are capable of doing, but they have a qualification that may be a little more polished than yours. You got it! If they talked crazy, so would I.

Remember that it's not always your knowledge of the job you possess that determines if you are fit for the job. I realized it was time to leave, and I must say I was offered a nice package when I stated that I needed to move on to a different pasture. I received my check for over six months, and then I was able to apply for unemployment. The whole time I was receiving my full check and benefits, I was in school studying to be a medical office assistant (MOA). I am glad to say I was writing a journal during that time, and it allowed me to see and study myself, and I graduated with honors. I started looking at myself from a different perspective.

I have always been active in church, even before my teenage years, but I can remember only one sermon from that era. It dealt with the Ten Commandments, and each one was explained in its entirety. Two commandments caught my attention: (1) Thou shall honor your father and your mother, and (2) thou shall not commit adultery. I didn't think about or pay any more attention to the rest of the commandments. (I was in elementary school at that time of my life.)

When I moved to Charlotte and my son was about ten years old, I joined Faith Christian Methodist Episcopal Church after being in Charlotte for about six months. I did attend another one of our churches, but I felt lost in the large membership. I was used to my home churches, and Faith CME was a new church in the Hidden Valley area with a smaller membership. I joined under the second pastor assigned to the church. I remember many of the sermons preached. The church was and is still a Bible-based teaching church. What caught my attention about the sermons was the fact that I was introduced more to the New Testament. But when the sermon was preached from James 3, I was all ears because I could relate to the danger of the tongue. I had no idea that was in the Bible. (The good Lord didn't strike me dead because of my mouth.)

I still didn't have the right relationship with God. I just heard some good preaching. My heart wasn't quite there yet, which meant neither was my tongue. But I will say that it kept me in check. I would start waiting to see if a comment or response was necessary. Don't get me wrong. If someone said something that I took to be offensive, I would speak my mind. I felt guilty about what I would say, but I did ask God to set a watch over my mouth and help me say things that would glorify His name.

I would be lying if I said nothing bothers me when something is said that doesn't sit well with me. I have to stop and look at what was said, and I have to remember that there is still a thin line between heaven and hell. But the following verses remind me that I have to be careful with what I put in my heart and mind.

Proverbs 21:23 says,

> *Whoso keepeth his mouth and his tongue keepeth his soul from troubles.*

Matthew 12:33–37 (NIV) says,

> *Make a tree good and its fruit will be good, or make a tree bad and its fruit will be bad, for a tree is recognized by its fruit. You brood of vipers, how can you who are evil say anything good? For out of the overflow of the heart the mouth speaks. The good man brings good things out of the good stored up in him, and the evil man brings evil things out of the evil stored up in him. But I tell you that men will have to give account on the day of the judgment for every careless word they have spoken. For by your words you will be condemned.*

Here, we can see in the above scripture how careful we need to be when we are communicating with people. This scripture teaches the following:

1. Our words can speak power.
2. Our character is known by the words we speak.
3. Our words determined our reward and judgment.
4. Remember that a tree is known by the fruit it bears.
5. Our words determine our final destination—heaven or hell.

James 3 reminds us to use wise words to accomplish what God would have us do and be in life.

In conclusion, when others say, *I remember when…*, ignore it because God knows your heart. I am sure some of my family members remember or know me for the way I used to be. I am reminded of the gospel song that says, "I won't go back, can't go back to the way it used to be." What the enemies did against me, God has turned around for me. *My mother was right. My mouth spoke death to my flesh.*

Now I will use my tongue to speak death to anyone who doesn't believe in God's Word and to those who will hear the true Word of God. I remember in my thirties, when I went to the doctor, describing funny butterflies in my chest. Immediately, he ordered an EKG. He didn't find anything seriously wrong but said that if it continued, he would have to give me medication for it. At thirty, I said to myself, "Not here." He suggested that when it happens again, I should hold my breath for a few seconds, and it will slow down the heart.

When someone says ugly or unnecessary things to you, do as the doctor suggested to me. Just hold your breath for a few seconds. We will call this verbal restraint. So rather than say something you may regret, just pause and think about whether you would be embarrassed by what you might say.

Before speaking, give the situation to God.

The Hat of a Preacher's Wife

When I was in elementary school and would see the preacher's wife, I would stare at her because she was always wearing a pretty dress and a matching hat. The hat mostly caught my attention because it was usually large and sometimes had big flowers or a big feather on it. I thought that ministers' wives were very special people because of their spouses. (In this era, we call them ministers' spouses because there are just as many female ministers as there are male.) Church people seemed to have treated her with deep respect. When I think about it, women during that era wore hats to church all the time. It didn't matter if it was the same one or not; they wore some form of head covering. Even I had to wear a hat to church. My mother was a PK (a.k.a. preacher's kid), and I had no choice because she was taught that it's appropriate to wear a hat to church. In my young years, I had to wear matching hats, shoes, and gloves—not just at Easter but every Sunday. My hat was black, and my favorite shoes were black patent leather. I love to wear my black patent leather heels now.

If there was a special dress code of ethics for the ministers' spouses, I would probably be out of order and a disgrace to my mother if she knew how I dress now. We tend to say things in the form of metaphor, like, "If my mother knew how I dress now, she would *turn over in her grave.*" Well, if that were true, I guess my mother would be a "spinner." She would probably be disappointed that I don't care to wear hats.

I remember when I was working for an ophthalmologist, two family friends came in for their appointments. On the way out, they said to me that they heard I was going to marry a preacher. I said, surprisingly, "Yes, I am."

The one who was a minister's spouse said, "Don't forget to get you some nice hats."

I told her that indeed I would get some nice hats in Mount Holly (my hometown).

She asked, "Where are you going to find nice hats in Mount Holly?"

I said, "Oh! Easy! From my sister's closet. She has many choices."

She said, "Okay, you are still Lorraine."

We both smiled, and she shook her head and said, "If that's your best choice, go ahead."

We both laughed and said goodbye. We talked often, but it was usually about writing. She and I both like to write. If you wonder if the hat conversation occurred, the answer is yes, and I reminded her where I got hats when I needed one for a special occasion.

I rarely—and I mean very rarely—wear a hat. I'm going to use my son's excuse about changes; he says it's a different generation. My comeback is, "Who made it different?"

Several weeks after I started writing this article, I saw the video of a virtual hat show sponsored by the Winston-Salem/Greenville Ministers' Spouses District. Unfortunately, I wasn't able to participate because of an unexpected obligation. (I was able to watch on Zoom.) A widow in the district gave a brief history of the importance of African American women wearing hats. OH, BOY! That really got my attention, and so I did some deep studying about hats and African American women. (PS. I hated history when I was in school, but the older I became, the more I enjoyed it.) I must say that the history wearing hat wasn't about fashion; it was all about what it represented.

Wearing the hats was to honor our God. This tradition goes as far back as slavery. The hats represented spiritual and cultural importance. I checked my Bible Dictionary about head covering, and it referred me to 1 Corinthians 11:5–6 (KJV), which confirmed that the head covering of a woman isn't just a fashion statement but a spiritual statement.

But every woman that prayeth or prophesieth with her head uncovered, dishonoureth her head:

for that is even all one as if she were shaven. For if the woman be not covered, let her also be shorn (an important part of the woman that has been removed completely): but if it be a shame for a woman to be shorn or shaven, let her be covered.

    I remember years ago that the Stewardesses at Faith CME Church would make sure on the first Sunday when we had Communion that no woman would be served without some form of covering on their head. The Stewardesses on duty at the altar would give women (who had no head covering) a Kleenex, or they would place it on their heads. I made my head covering from a piece of lace material. I took a plate and cut out my hat. I would keep it in my Bible so I would be prepared for Communion on every first Sunday. No women were offended when they had a tissue placed on their heads.

    During this era, women received communion at our church without head coverings. I know that the president of the Stewardesses board at Faith CME during that time took the Bible for what it literally said. I don't know if our *Discipline* ever stated that it was required. The changing of the head covering while taking communion had a lot to do with the assignments of the pastors.

    It seems that being women of color, especially African Americans, we have to try harder to prove our self-worth, who we are, and whose we are. While studying sociology, I learned that even your handwriting says a lot about your personality. The same goes for the wearing of fancy and sometimes large hats.

    Reading about slave women and their wearing of hats made them feel good about themselves, especially after a hard week's work. But you know, the slave owners didn't like the idea of them dressing up, wearing their fancy hats, and feeling so jubilant, singing and giving praise to God. So they decided to degrade them by shaving their hair off. But because of their spiritual and cultural beliefs, they started making head wraps with cloth. (Ain't God good? He made it possible for them to keep their faith and still honor Him.) Here, again, is another way African American women had to prove themselves. The hats were a symbol of an expression of triumph over the struggles they faced. The hat was their crown. The women would still wear fancy straw hats in the field. Well, there is an old saying, "You can't keep a good woman down." It reminds me of a book I read years ago that said, "Some things a strong woman doesn't give up and one was their power." Our strong, Black older women found their power in wearing their crowns.

After I married and wasn't at home with my mother, I didn't wear a hat anymore. If my memory serves me well, I only wore hats in my adult life when I became a minister's spouse, and we wore them for special programs during annual conferences and homegoing services. We wore them only by choice. We had several who enjoyed wearing hats.

In reading the history behind African American women and the wearing of hats, I learned that the young ladies during the sixties refused to wear hats because they learned they (the hats) represented oppression. But when they became Elders in the church, they started wearing hats, even though they previously ridiculed those who continued wearing the hats. A lot of different religions require elder women in certain positions to wear hats.

When I look around in my church, there are a few older women still wearing hats. I remember one of the ladies in the church asking me where my hat was. I said, "What hat?" I told her she would see me in a hat at church in the winter if it was cold.

My youngest sister wouldn't think about going to church without a hat. She remembered how we were taught, but most of all, she likes hats and nice clothes. I am glad that she likes hats and takes really good care of them, so I have a nice hat to wear when I decide to wear one for a special occasion.

Well, I guess I need to start wearing hats, especially after reading the history behind our ancestors' purpose for wearing them and seeing the virtual hat show.

Since we have been out of church for about two years, I've had no reason to purchase or visit my sister's closet, but I guess I need to start looking for hat sales.

Well, since I started writing this book, I have changed my taste in clothing. I like the vintage and have always loved the Roaring

Twenties styles, and the hats make the difference. I have changed my hairstyle, so a big hat would cover my face too much since my hair is short.

Thanks, Mom, for showing me there was a reason for my wearing a hat.

How Can Caring Too Much Be Painful

WHEN I THINK about how Jesus cares so much for us yet was betrayed and crucified to reconcile us back to the right relationship with the Lord because of our sins, I can see and understand how caring so much can be painful. On the other side of the spectrum, I can relate from my personal experience how painful it can be.

Most of us are satisfied with our medical doctors and specialists. We feel they are doing a great job caring for us.

I was born into a large family. I was the tenth out of twelve, to be exact. We were raised in a very close-knit family. It sounds like a very crowded home, but had about four, at the most, children at home. After graduation, some got married, some went off to college, and three of the guys joined the military.

When any member of the family became ill, we would all be concerned. We always had a family member who would be contacted to inform the family of the circumstances and the condition of our loved one's progress. My family member had a few little things going on that the doctor was concerned about and wanted to get a specialist to see what the diagnosis could be. The specialist needed was an ophthalmologist. While talking to the caregiver, I made a comment that I wished he could see my ophthalmologist because of my love for my family member and memory of our mother's loss of sight because her doctor wasn't a specialist, nor did he know how to treat what he thought she had.

The specialist I worked for was well-known for his knowledge of an eye disease that other doctors in the area had no knowledge of.

The closest doctor who had the same knowledge was in Baltimore, Maryland. He had patients referred to him as far away as the east coast of North Carolina and Florida. Doctors from Duke University Hospital, Baptist Hospital, and other facilities referred patients to him, so of course I wanted the best for my loved one.

Never would I have thought it would be taken out of context and blown up the way it was, especially by the people who lit the dynamite. Apparently, one of the two who took my caring for an insult decided to call a meeting with my siblings, except the ones who were ill, one other sibling, and a niece, who stated they didn't want any part of what my nephew was trying to do because it seemed as if someone was trying to stir up the "devil's workshop."

I received a call from my son, who told me about the call and the awful things said about me. He said there must be something going on because one of the siblings on the phone was a shock to him. I was devastated. I cried so hard that I told him that if he believed those lies, then he didn't need to even consider me his mom anymore and that I didn't have to be part of the family that allowed someone to tell them things that had nothing to do with the sick family member. My husband was ready to make a call and set the records straight, and he informed my son that those were all lies and that he would not stand for anyone to hurt me with such untrue statements.

All my life, we have never had anything like this occur in our family between siblings. I felt like dying, and no one had to be concerned because it seemed as though I was the odd crayon in the box. But to God be the glory that I had matured in my life and that the tracks that Satan had running in my mind didn't make it to my mouth because I would be no better than those who may not have known the following:

> *Moreover if thy brother shall trespass against thee, go and tell him his fault between thee and him alone: if he hear thee, thou hast gained thy brother. But if he will not hear thee, then take with thee one or two more, that in the mouth of two or three witnesses every word may be established. And if he shall*

WHO ARE THE CHRISTIANS IN THE CHURCH?

neglect to hear them, tell it to the church: but if he neglect to hear the church, let him be unto thee as a pagan [a person holding religious beliefs other than those of the main world religions] and a publican (a tax collector). (NIV)

This situation is another example of how we misuse God's Word because verse 15 was skipped. Two days later, I called my ill family member and made the situation known and how it badly hurt me. The first comment he made was that we will pray about this and the truth will be revealed about the whole issue, or better yet, the justification of such a mess. It was a very shocking moment when informed of who instigated the situation. I was told, "Don't ever feel as if you aren't important to the family." Words of comfort were spoken when they said to me, "God will take care of the situation."

Several months later, we were coming up on our almost fiftieth year of celebrating our annual family Christmas dinner. Everyone was glad to see each other as usual, as if nothing had happened. I was still hurting because I had never experienced such a wounded heart. I made a promise that I would let go and let God. If the truth be told, I had not forgiven them because I was still hurt.

It has been said many times that the people who hurt you the most are your family and loved ones. That's because we put so much trust and love in them, and we are so close to them that when we are betrayed, it digs deep into the heart. It caused me, at that period, distrust, and it forced me to wonder what steps or directions I should take from here. But with constant prayer, I thank God for a new mindset that's totally different from the way I once would have responded.

So when that betrayal demon tries to raise its head, I remember the saying, "It takes two to tangle." If you don't give it space in your head, then it will just go away because no one likes to be ignored. I treat it like an email I know isn't important to me. I hit the delete key and then went to the trash file and emptied it from that file. Remember that you are in control of who and what affects you.

LORRAINE McCULLOUGH-BROWN

Food for thought

> The weak can never forgive. Forgiveness is the attribute of the strong. (Mahatma Gandhi)

> Our ultimate freedom is the right and power to decide how anybody or anything outside ourselves will affect us. (Stephen R. Covey)

The CME Church
Injustice (Part 1)

I MENTIONED INJUSTICE ACTS in the churches in a previous chapter. So I want you to understand that some of you may think I'm being very harsh, and some may say that I am lying or angry. No! I am *so* far past the angry stage.

Before my marriage to Rev. Jack Brown Jr., several ministers' spouses shared their feelings and experiences as to their sudden new church assignments. Many sudden charges (new church assignments) were caused by many of the members who did not like the changes made by their present pastor. They stated that so many churches disregard the *Discipline*. So when a new pastor comes in and notices that the order is not familiar based on previous assignments that *were* in accordance with the *Discipline*, this brings about a rip.

They wanted to know why the pastor found it necessary to make changes since they had been doing it that way for years and it had been working okay for them. They found the *Discipline* not necessary to operate and give praise to God. Examples of the Christian Methodist Episcopal Church's doctrine are as follows: (1) *order of service to follow*, (2) *type of songs to be sung at certain times during services and when to sing them*, (3) *limiting the number of stanzas to sing at one time*. I could go on with many other CME doctrines, but I just wanted to name a few that could cause a ripple in the churches.

If you want to hear about a really heavy situation that can cause a big ripple in a church, it is when the pastor learns that there is some dishonesty on the steward board. (This is not an issue I wish to expound upon because of its sensitivity. I wasn't aware until he audited the books, and later, I learned that two members of the board knew and told Rev. Brown but didn't tell me because they wanted the people to correct what they were doing. At this point, I resigned because my trust had been betrayed.

When Rev. Jack Brown Jr. was assigned to Faith CME, he first met with his officers and members. He shared his expectations of each member and the officers. He also read what was required of each officer, each department, and the auxiliary. At that moment, no questions were asked pertaining to the meeting. A funny thing was that I was the chairman of the steward board (LOL).

In most situations, when a new pastor is assigned to a church, the steward board or chairperson is responsible for making sure a reservation for a hotel room is made for the pastor and his family. A welcome basket is usually prepared with snacks and some beverages. Well, guess who was left to show the new pastor around Charlotte and where to find restaurants with home-cooked meals? He was specific about the types of foods he liked. Yes, it was me. My guy friend was coming by my house before he left for work, but I was a tour guide for the pastor. He wanted to see where the parsonage was and how to get to the church from there. He couldn't go inside because, according to our *Discipline*, the previous pastor and family had thirty days to evacuate.

Just a little history behind Rev. Jack, who accepted his calling into the ministry. He was assigned under Bishop Coles to the sixth Episcopal District in the South Georgia Annual Conference. Upon entering the ministry out of Hadley CME Church, he attended his first conference in Brunswick, Georgia, where he had his first examination. Dr. Amos Ryce was the chairperson. Some of the board members were Maceo Pettigrew from the CME Publishing House, Rev. John H. Malone, Rev. U. A. Hammonds, and Rev. James Hazel. Each advised him to always check the church's property for any lien holds or loans and to always have someone audit your books. Very few people were aware that Rev. Brown attended the FBI Academy for arson investigations, which included a lot of paperwork and background investigations. Going through the training under the leadership of the examination board, two things stood out. These two things were as follows: (1) audit your books; (2) and check the deeds of the church's properties.

Rev. Jack discovered that there had been two unethical situations that had occurred prior to his assignment to the church. Being in compliance with the *Discipline*, these two issues were reported to his immediate supervisor. They met with the CEO (bishop) of our episcopacy. Because of the circumstances, the CEO stated that he would see that it was corrected. *The "elephant in the room,"* who was dealing with the deed, was seen only from the higher echelon's perspective.

This "elephant in the room" still exists, but he has been whitewashed by the audit of the book. (This is not an issue I wish to expound upon because of its sensitivity. I wasn't aware the books had been audited until I learned that two members of the board knew of the unethical practice and told Rev. Brown, but they didn't tell me because they wanted the people to correct what they were doing.) At that point, I resigned because my trust in my staff had been betrayed. Rev. Brown tried to handle the situation *delicately*, but it didn't materialize.

After two years at Faith CME Church, Rev. Brown was reassigned. Yes, it had a lot to do with him following what he was taught under the leadership of the examination board. It seems that pastors have to turn blind eyes to unethical actions that are against the general rules of the CME Church. Under the general rules in the *Book of Discipline*, Article 126 states that "borrowing without a probability of paying or taking up goods without a probability of paying for them" is a violation of the general rules of the church. OH! Maybe there is a gray area in that article that "states it's based on the pastor who discovered it or brought it to the proper channel to rectify the issue, or that pastor is causing trouble."

After two years of being reassigned from Faith CME, I became Lorraine Brown. I must say, I never thought that was in the making. When my husband asked me, I told him that I didn't like him like that. But evidently, I didn't know what I was talking about. This I know: What God puts together, no man can put asunder.

LORRAINE McCULLOUGH-BROWN

Food for thought

> *If you are neutral in situations of injustice, you have chosen the side of the oppressor. If an elephant has its foot on the tail of a mouse and you say that you are neutral, the mouse will not appreciate your neutrality. (Desmond Tutu)*

Becoming a Minister's Spouse

In a previous article, I spoke of my admiration for a preacher's wife. Now they are called minister's spouses because there are just as many female pastors/ministers as males. Now that I am a minister's spouse, I've learned that being a spouse is not a glorified position. As a minister's spouse, I have also learned that there seem to be separate expectations for a minister's spouse versus other women in church.

If we aren't careful, we will lose our identity and will only be called or known as the pastor's spouse. Would it make me less important if I was called Mrs. Lorraine Brown? Does conjuring up the title (lady) for me make me more important or a step above other women in our churches? Or should I look at it as part of being in an organization that shares respect for one another?

Don't misconstrue my point here. My husband seems to think I overthink words. He reminded me that English is the hardest language to understand—*that, I know*—and the definition of a word changes often. The word I am struggling with is "lady." Now I must admit that there is a very astute person of whom I think highly, and definitely her picture can be used to show or demonstrate a "lady," especially after I read the definition from *Merriam-Webster's Dictionary*. I teased her that she was such a smooth talker and that she could sell swamp land and say that it was "waterfront property." But I have learned that even a lady can make an error. It has been proven.

On the national level, spouses are usually referred to as ladies instead of missus or the like. On another level, usually district level, spouses are fine with being referred to as *sisters*. To be honest, I am comfortable being called Sister Lorraine. I feel that special expectations are expected of me if I am called a *lady* versus a *sister*. You see if I am called *sister*, I feel that I am really part of you as a close friend or a sister in Christ. I feel that you are less likely to judge me and will accept me just as I am, with my flaws. There are times when I know that I stumble. Being called a sister doesn't make me feel as though I am being put on a pedestal, but as though I am being loved. I also feel that if I stumble, I won't have far to fall.

Another reason for my struggle with being called a *lady* is a conversation I overheard among some spouses. I witnessed their demeanor toward other ministers' spouses, which wasn't Christlike. A *lady* is a title, but it doesn't exemplify a Christian. Don't misconstrue what I am saying. I am not judging anyone, but some of the actions that spouses displayed toward one another didn't represent those of a Christian or a *lady*. The one title we all should work hard at is being Christians. As Christians, we should both think and behave like Jesus. So please, call me Sister Brown.

The one lesson I learned quickly from the first church I attended as a minister's spouse was not to attend church conferences. During the years I was single, I didn't have a margin in my mouth. This meant I would come right back at yah! I knew too well what I was hearing during that church conference, out of the abundance of my heart. The mouth *"would speak,"* and *no, it wouldn't be pretty.*

As a spouse, a few other spouses and I have shared how we tend to feel that it's our responsibility to protect our spouses. Jack and I did talk about my feelings, and he assured me that God didn't call him into the ministry without watching over him. I listened to him very clearly, but I still felt like I wanted to help God. (I know God didn't need my help, but my heart and my love for my husband caused me to still struggle with the thought of how arrogant some people were and still are.)

I must say I shed many tears with my first church assignment because all of this was new to me. I wanted to go back to my home church, where I felt comfortable, but that didn't go over well. One day, Jack and I were on our way to Charlotte from Chesnee, South Carolina. I was driving. The song "Lord, It's in Your Hand" was playing on the radio, and I started having heart palpitations, which meant

WHO ARE THE CHRISTIANS IN THE CHURCH?

I was experiencing my heart racing, pounding, fluttering, and skipping a beat. I started streaming, and Jack said, "What's going on?"

All I could do was scream and cry. I had to pull over to the side of the road because I was hysterical. My hands felt as if they were glued to the steering wheel. I couldn't talk, and Jack tried to calm me down. Before he could get me calm, the third verse of the song said, *"Temptations comes in every way, but in my heart Jesus, that's where you must stay, cause living down here day to day, it gets* rough *it gets tough for me Jesus, but to you I pray."*

I was at a point where praying got hard. Oh, my soul! When he finally got me out of the driver's seat and calm enough to talk, I shared how that song was telling me how I felt. He reminded me that I am trying too hard not to be the real me, but who I think I'm supposed to be, and how am I supposed to act? He said I needed to be the person he fell in love with who had no problem expressing her real feelings, "but not as harshly," and he laughed. I felt better after we talked. It's been said, and we often say, that God will send us through the valley because He knows our strength or what we can bear. I wished I had a "heads-up" about the journey I was embarking on as a minister's spouse.

I made it through the valley, even with the trials. I also have scars to remind me that it was worth the battles for my growth. After much prayer and much power, I became a youth Sunday school teacher, and I started teaching midday Bible study. The ladies mostly came during midday, and those who were still working came at night when Jack was teaching.

I thank God for Terry, Mildred, and Chris McIntyre, as well as Rev. Doris Landrum and her late husband, Boyce Landrum. They were very cordial, and they showed so much love and appreciation toward us. As of this date, after over twenty years, we are still extremely close, like family should be.

With their spiritual and financial support, I learned my strengths: *self-control, courage, honesty, sincerity, hope, and unselfishness.* It didn't happen overnight. Reading *James 3* taught me to restrain my tongue from saying that *would not honor God. I remember learning the "three-second verbal rule"—know the consequences and allow God to do what He does best.*

When I was in the sixth grade, we had devotion before the beginning of class. Each student had to say or read a Bible verse. I chose *Proverbs 15:1*, *"A soft answer turneth away wrath, but grievous words stir up anger."* I never forgot that scripture because I clearly understood what it meant. When you can relate to something, it tends to stay with you. No, I didn't practice it well. Later in life, I got over myself and realized every comment doesn't need a response. I learned that sometimes some things are better left unsaid. Trust me, it was a long row to hoe. (This meant that I had something difficult to deal with, and it took a long time to accomplish.) Thank God for having favor over my life.

Being the president of the Carolina Regional Ministers' Spouses taught me when and what to say at difficult times. It wasn't a mistake for me to be in that position, but it was part of the path that I had to walk for my spiritual growth. God placed me there not so much for others but for myself.

A well-known quote about self-control that rings a bell with me was written by Morgan Freeman.

> *Self-control is strength. Calmness is mastery. You have to get to a point where your mood doesn't shift based on the insignificant actions of someone else. Don't allow others to control the direction of your life. Don't allow your emotions to overpower your intelligence.*

Surely, it sounds so pretty, but I didn't do a great job of applying it at times.

With *courage*, I think of bravery, confidence, and the ability to support someone else. I know I can't change some things, and I have to learn to accept the things I cannot change. I must admit that it's not always that easy. If I see someone walking down the wrong path and I know that it is wrong, as a child of God, I feel that I am obligated to witness to them. I may or may not see the change, but it's okay as long as the effect takes place because I am not doing it for myself. Aristotle, known as a Greek philosopher, said that *"courage involves pain, and is justly praised; for it is harder to face what is painful than to abstain from what is pleasant."*

Philippians 1:6 reminded me to be confident, knowing that God began a good work in me and that He will carry it on to completion until the day of Christ Jesus.

As a child of God who confesses to being a Christian, I know that I must be *honest* with myself as well as with others. My honesty reflects who I am, and it shows in my character. If I don't live the life of a Christlike person, then I will be lying about who I really am.

When I married Jack, I thought I had to change who I was and be who other people thought I should be. I thought I had to always be prepared to recite a scripture during a simple conversation. He reminded me that God called him into the ministry and not me, and I should be who God made me to be.

Proverbs 12:22 says, *"The Lord detests lying lips, but he delights in men who are truthful."* I have to be real. It's less painful when you're yourself and not pretentious. Regardless of who you are and where you are worshiping as the pastor's wife, honesty is the best way to present yourself. Honesty guides good people; dishonesty destroys treacherous people (Proverbs 11:3).

When I think about being sincere, I recall when I became a minister's spouse I felt I would be observed more than before becoming a spouse, and I knew I needed to make a change in my spiritual walk. I would criticize some people's ways or acts that were so out of character for a Christian. Then it hit me that I had some non-Christian characteristics as well.

The thought of some of my previous sins makes my body shiver. No, I'm not sin-free. When I became older and started studying the Word again, I realized that I had to be sincere and not fake my true feelings and service to God. I know I have to be genuine about my spiritual walk. I am glad our God is a forgiving God because some hurtful thoughts and lies they told on me that have come to mind were from people who I felt were my friends and whom I dearly loved.

I was hurt, but I asked God to forgive me for my angry thoughts and to bless them even if the truth wasn't told.

I was reminded by my pastor, Rev. Dr. Sandra H. Gripper, who stated, "Lo [that's what she calls me], if you only knew how people have lied and treated me. If it wasn't for God, I may have wanted to get them in a corner and maybe make matters worse. Pray and keep moving, especially when the truth is known."

I have learned to show my sincerity for my love for God by forgiving and being about the calling He has on my life. I must avoid wickedness, continue to show love for others, and show opposition to fleshy wisdom. When I learned to accept the plans God has for me, my life seemed easier. Yes, I have questioned God. Yes, I questioned why He ordered these steps for my life. Yes, I wanted to just give up and say, "I quit!"

After many conversations with God and my husband, I lost both battles. We've all probably heard about the way a diamond is formed. It is formed from carbon deposits deep within the earth, which are subjected to temperature and pressure. There is no way of knowing how long it takes to form. Some scientists have said it may materialize in days, weeks, or months. I, too, was formed from dirt, but look where He has brought me!

I am seventy-seven now, and it has taken a lot of years to get where I am with my Christian walk. I have been under a lot of pressure and heat, like a diamond in the rough. I know that there have been times when there have been some nicks and cracks that have caused me to have imperfections in my life. But as long as I keep my eyes on the prize, heaven will be my home.

After carefully studying God's Word about sincerity, I learned that it is simply saying, "We must walk the walk and not just talk the talk." If we confess to be Christians, then we must study to show ourselves in such a manner that we will get God's approval of how we are representing who we confess to be. Genuine sincerity is described very clearly *in Philippians 1:10*: *"That yea may approve things that are excellent; that ye may be sincere and without offence till the day of Christ."*

WHO ARE THE CHRISTIANS IN THE CHURCH?

When I thought about hope, my mind reflected on a quote by Michelle Obama:

> *You may not always have a comfortable life and you will not always be able to solve all of the world's problems at once but don't ever underestimate the importance you can have because history has shown us courage can be contagious and hope can take on a life of its own.*

I must say it hasn't been easy for me to accept unmeasurable disappointments in my life and try to keep hope alive. Sometimes, life seemed very dim. My mother made our lives appear as if everything was going well. She never complained or compared our lives with those of another household. I learned from my mother how to make a way out of what seemed like an impossible situation.

When the winter weather was bad, our father's job was affected since he was in construction. The refrigerator may not have had plenty, but she could make a meal out of what was there, and we were never hungry from a lack of food. As my youngest sister, Cynthia, would say, "Oatmeal is better than no meal." As a child, I never worried about not having. My mother made provisions for us to have what we needed. We didn't try to live beyond our means. We knew how the money was flowing in the house.

When I look back over my life, I never thought we were classified as a low-income or middle-income family. As a mother—and at one point, a single parent—a grandmother, a great-grandmother, and really knowing God, I know how she made sure we had nice clothes, shoes, and other items we needed for school. I am wearing my high school class ring from 1963 that cost about twenty-five dollars, and my mother paid so much weekly to assure me that I would get one just like my classmates.

My mother was well-known in the neighborhood, the department stores, and other businesses in Mount Holly, North Carolina, where I was born. We could go to Paul Derr Department Store and get clothes and walk out of the store with the clothes on, and my mother was allowed to pay for the clothes when she could. Of course, she had put a limit on the cost of the outfit. My mom did an awesome job raising us. She instilled values in us at a very young age. It's good to know that hope means God is for us. Thank God for the values we were taught because they were valuable instructional measures that assisted us in our lives. Thank you, Mama.

When I think of unselfishness, I love the scripture Matthew 25:40 (KJV): "And the King shall answer and say unto them, Verily I say unto you, Inasmuch as ye have done it unto one of the least of these my brethren, ye have done it unto me."

As a child, I learned to do for others by watching my mother. I learned a lot from my mother, and I guess it was part of the steps God ordered for my life. I enjoy giving, whether it's encouragement a thank-you card, or one that says, "Thinking of you." I enjoy giving when I can, whether it's small or large.

When I give, I don't expect anything in return. A member of one of Jack's charges (churches) said that we were so generous with our time and talents. She stated that if she and her husband were to go on vacation and they had a store, they would not ask us to manage the store while they were gone because they felt we would give all the items away.

Jokingly, I said, "The more we give, the more He'll give to you." Maybe not! I am sure that if there was someone who may have been a dollar short and it was something they really wanted, I would give them the dollar.

As a personal project, during the COVID-19 shutdown of rehab facilities, I made cards to deliver to two centers. One was near my church (Hunter Woods Rehab in Charlotte, North Carolina), and the other was about forty-five miles away from where I live, which is in Monroe, North Carolina (Monroe Rehabilitation).

Jack and I have since had a home built in Monroe, North Carolina. Both event planners for the facilities were happy that I thought of their facilities. I can easily drop them off near the church on Monroe. I must say it requires a lot of my time, but the thought of the isolated residents gives me enough energy to keep pushing. I don't have a family member in either one of the facilities, and it still doesn't matter. After my husband's extensive back surgery, I must say it was a struggle trying to care for him, write my book, and make cards. Of course, you know who took preference.

I thank God for a very close and dear friend, Sylvia, who lived on the same floor with us when we lived in Belmont, North Carolina. She knows that I enjoy giving and sending cards. She donated to several nonprofit organizations, and they sent her cards all year. She gives them to me, and it really helps a lot. During the Christmas holiday, she gave me plenty of cards, and I didn't have to make any. This allowed time to write, and at this point, my husband didn't need as much assistance getting dressed. (Praise God for His healing!)

I am motivated with joy to do the cards for the isolated residents in the rehab facilities. Once again, another season was fast approaching, and I felt overwhelmed, so I reached out to my church, mainly because I was going to send cards to some of the church's homebound seniors. I knew I wasn't going to try to make enough for both facilities timely. To my surprise, only one young lady, Shanna Greene, donated toward the purchase of the cards. I was disappointed, but I realized what might be valuable to me might not be to others. I thank God that I was able to deliver cards to both facilities and the homebound members of the church. Each card that I send is signed with the name of the church, the address, and the pastor's name. I don't do the cards for me but for the isolated residents.

A songwriter said, "*I give myself away so you can use me.*" That's how I feel when I do what I do. I wear myself down sometimes, and I feel like crying because my body is so tired, but I keep on pushing because I love seniors, and I always have, even as a very young child.

Philippians 2:3–4 (NIV) states, "Do nothing out of selfish ambition or vain conceit, but in humility consider others better than yourselves. Each of you should look not only to your own interests but also to the interests of others." Ways of showing unselfishness can be observed simply by sending someone a card and a handwritten letter (not an email), or a brief phone call. Jack and I have picked up the tab for someone at a restaurant; even just kind words of encouragement to someone we meet in a store or at the grocery store, or even when we get a telemarketer call, they say *thanks* real fast. Any of the suggestions will never be forgotten.

Remember God's word in Matthew 25:40 (previously stated).

Assignment Meant to Be an Insult
Injustice (Part 2)

God Turned into a Blessing

IF YOU RECALL in another chapter, I spoke of some ministers' spouses who stated that if a pastor comes in with changes or new ideas, it can and will cause members to become irritated, or shall I say, it causes a rip. Rather than churches sharing their concerns with the pastors, which is part of the way it is to be handled according to our *Discipline*, they prefer calling the order (Elder) or the bishop (based on who is in office during that time) to complain about the pastor.

Many churches have been known to say we aren't going to pay all of our assessments (those are funds or assets of each church used to pay for operating expenses and commitments to support our colleges, bishop salaries, travel funds, and the like). It does play a part in determining whether or not they will receive their next assignments. Jack was well-known for seeing that the churches he pastored met their obligations. When Jack was at Faith CME and brought two issues before the Elder, the bishop especially caused a ripple. *The elephant in the room* (which I spoke of earlier) had a lot to do with his being transferred to a smaller church, and his salary was cut by over four hundred and fifty dollars. He was to live in a parsonage that was infested with insects, with a rotten bathroom floor, and an inoperative kitchen. He never mumbled a word. One thing in his favor was that he could live in the parsonage in Charlotte for thirty days, which he and three other men from Faith CME renovated when he was first assigned there.

When I was asking some questions about the past for my book, I felt his hurt. He asked if we could discontinue the conversation. While traveling the distance from Charlotte to Union Mills, North Carolina, the men and one ninety-year-old lady were working on the parsonage while he was in Charlotte. He would go up early every Tuesday morning because of his tutorial classes and on Thursdays to work on the parsonage with the members, and he had Bible study on Wednesday nights. He traveled back to Charlotte on Thursday.

The church loved him. The men had an awesome bond with him. They would come by the parsonage and say they knew he would have a lot of breakfast food cooked, and they didn't want it to go to waste (LOL). The men would contact one another and meet at the parsonage. They would eat breakfast and discuss the financial and physical needs of the church. Sometimes they would come by just to sit on the porch, rock in the rocking chairs, and just talk. Sometimes they would be blessed with homemade fried apple pies from the oldest member of the church. Now this is when the reverend could act indignant because he didn't want to share those fried apple pies.

Jack was told by his parents to speak to other people in passing, whether while walking down the sidewalk or in a store. His parents told him it wasn't relevant if they didn't respond. I am saying this to say that he was eating lunch or breakfast in one of the restaurants in the area (if I were with him, I would've said find me a Burger King or a McDonald's, but we weren't married) if you catch my drift. This was a small town, and they probably knew each other and recognized Jack as a stranger in town. I am trying to say something without showing prejudice. Okay!

Well, Jack would go where food was served. When he went in and sat at the bar, he spoke to the gentleman who was sitting beside him, introduced himself as Rev. Jack Brown, and told him the name of the church he was pastoring in the neighborhood. The gentleman introduced himself as Jack also and said, "I've heard from your member Robert [a retired fireman)]. What a great job you are doing, and we are glad to have you here in our town." The gentleman later said,

WHO ARE THE CHRISTIANS IN THE CHURCH?

"I am the mayor. If there's anything or a way we can help, please let me or Robert know."

Jack didn't hesitate to tell him that the men of the church talked about organizing a *summer enrichment program*. He explained that the purpose of the program was to aid students who needed assistance with their classes as well as to teach them about life changes in this world. There were special classes for each gender. The mayor stated there was an older school used for minor programs that needed some repairs, and he informed him that he and the men of the church were welcome to look at it.

After checking the condition of the property, they met with the mayor and a member of the Board of City Commissioners, and they told them what they observed. The elderly lady who was with the City Commissioner was a former executive for AT&T, and she stated that the only way the building could get a grant for repairs was if it was being used. So the church started having its tutorial program there and was awarded $225,000 for repairs to the roof and the bathrooms. There were days she would come and sit on the front porch of the patronage and talk about how she was excited about seeing the progress in all the children's lives and how their attitudes had changed. He gave credit to God, her, the men of the church, and all the volunteers who made it happen.

As the saying goes, "You never know when you are entertaining an angel," so we should always treat people with kindness and respect. Just think what Jack would've missed out on if he ignored the man sitting beside him. Words from *inspirekindness.com*, "*The world is full of kind people. If you can't find one, be one.*" Just a hello turned into a blessing for the community and Mount Pleasant Church CME Church.

After the completion of all necessary repairs, the *summer enrichment program* at the newly renovated school was announced in the local paper, reaching out for volunteers. It was so amazing how many volunteers came out to support this program. There were not only Black but also many White volunteers. The program was wonderful.

I admired three special ladies. One lady was ninety years old and from the church where Jack was preaching. She made sure they had desserts after their meals. A well-seasoned White retired home economics teacher showed them how to sew little things and what we call DIY for your home or self-made gifts. Our very own Rev. Dr. Lisa Reid, who at that time was Lisa Reid, showed them proper table etiquette. They were told the purpose of each eating instrument as well as how to fold napkins in different designs.

My understanding from Rev. Jack was that the young fellows were more interested in learning the etiquette than the young girls. He stated that they could reset the table and name the eating instrument very easily. (Just picture this from the crystal ball: the *young* girls standing around and holding onto each other, laughing, flinging their hair, and maybe criticizing the young fellows because they think it's too "girly" for young boys to enjoy learning about table etiquette.) Just saying and not judging anyone. I am just repeating that the fellows showed more interest. I was disappointed that I couldn't be part of it, but my job was short-staffed.

Well, conference time was fast approaching again. In the tutorial classes, they had to bring their report cards so Jack could see their progress. Gee, time flies when you are having fun. There was a young girl who attended the tutorial classes, and her mother was very concerned that her daughter was a hopeless case. That's a *no-no* around Jack. He believes everyone can learn if given a chance to prove themselves. Close to the end of school, she got her grades, and she flipped all of her classes to As. Jack and the staff learned that she had also received a scholarship to UNC Chapel Hill to study psychology. Months later, we saw her doing a commercial on television.

There was a young man whose mom thought he had a medical problem and needed to be on medication, but he enjoyed the attention he was receiving from the staff at tutorial. His grades turned around, and his Fs became Bs, and he changed his attitude toward school and decided to go to a nearby technical school.

They did a tour of a nearby gold mine and received help with transportation from Piney Ridge CME Church, which was nearby. Rev. Johnny Searight was the pastor at that time. During the summer enrichment program, Jack had to go to the annual conference.

He stated how the church blessed him financially to help with his expenses to attend the annual conference. Of course, they prayed that he would return. He told the men and the commissioner that if he didn't return, she should make sure the program continued. During the annual conference, he was assigned to Brooklyn CME Church in Chesnee, South Carolina.

Two weeks after his new assignment, he and I got married on August 17, 2002, at Helton Manor in Gastonia, North Carolina. The funny thing was that we paid the cost to use the building, and Jack had to get help cleaning it for our wedding. No, we didn't get a discount. We didn't let it bother us because it was just a minor hiccup. We thank God for the change that was about to happen in our lives together, and we just gave praise to our God.

A quote from Ida B. Wells says, "*The way to right wrongs is to turn the light of truth upon them.*"

Assignment to Brooklyn CME Church
Injustice (Part 3)

Brooklyn CME was the first church I attended as a minister's spouse. As I stated, I learned a lot about the *do*s and *don't*s of being the minister's spouse. After being there for several months, I stated that it was time to go back to my home church. You're talking about an insult to an injury when the order stated, after Jack's assignment to that church, "Don't mess this one up." Yes, this is a grown man who claims to be a Christlike person talking to another grown man in that manner. My husband just looked and didn't say a word. My tongue felt like it was stuck, and I knew I had to smile with chest pain. Yes, I had some words that I *knew* were mean, and I couldn't embarrass myself or my husband, nor did I need to pave my way to hell with the damage I could've caused.

Well, you know the story by now that my husband was assigned to a different church, which meant meeting with his members and most of all his steward board. He asked if there was any type of lien against the church. The steward chair appeared as though he didn't understand the question. So he asked, "Is there a loan against the church?" They answered no. When questioned about the church account and where the checkbook was kept, it got pretty quiet. A member of the steward board stated that the person who had the book wasn't present. He told the steward board member to please make sure the person was present with the checkbook on the next day, which was Sunday. That person showed up on Monday at the church with the book. They were confused as to why he needed all that information about the checking account. When the chair asked why he needed to see the checkbook, he told him that he needed to add his name to the account. The chair stated that no pastor's name had ever been on the checking account. Rev. Jack reminded him that he was assigned there as the pastor, which gives him the right to be listed on the account as well as see the steward's monthly reports. The chair was very adamant that Jack's name would not go on the account.

Rather than get worked up over that comment, the next day, Jack went to the bank with his charged assignment. He noticed a familiar face. He went to that teller, and he spoke to her because she was a member of the church. He told her that he needed to add his name to the church account and also needed records from the last five years of the account. She responded, "Sure, I can help you with that."

After receiving the information from the bank, he called a church conference to discuss some concerns he had. He asked the steward board for copies of the church's bills, and he reminded them of his request for the steward's church conference reports. The chair told him he didn't need to see the bills and asked what was so important about seeing the steward's reports because no one else asked to see them. His response to that statement was the fact that, as a pastor, it is his job to know what bills the church owes and that it's his business to know what funds come into the church.

The chair said that no other pastors asked for that information because they left it up to the steward board to pay the bills. Jack agreed with him that it was the steward board that paid the bills, but it's his business to know what was paid and when it was paid.

After going back and forth about who's on first and why that person is on second, Jack finally got copies of the steward board's reports several months later. Oh, by the way, he received them after someone stole his personal computer from his office that was given to him by a couple of church members. When word got out that the pastor's name was on the account and he had records going back as far as five years, it was very unnerving for some members of the board.

Well, the computer may have been stolen, but the bank statements weren't missing. After checking the statements against the steward's reports, many red flags were showing that they didn't match.

During a quarterly conference, the discrepancies between the steward's reports and the amount that was actually in the account were brought to the attention of the next order. One officer shouted out that my husband had misappropriated the funds if there was a discrepancy. A three-year audit didn't show any such accusations. (Just a reminder, Jack wasn't there then.) They were very adamant that there wasn't an error with the bank statements from the past. They would never accept the fact that the books had been audited and that what my husband reported was correct. They were still trying to find a way to accuse him of misusing the funds, and the next order went along with the members, even with the church's bank statements from five years ago and with the present statement.

You may have heard the old saying, "You're d—— if you do, and d—— if you don't." WHAT'S A PASTOR TO DO? The spouse of the higher-up told her husband that he was wrong for going along with those lies that they had accused my husband of. Several members of the church made it known that Rev. Brown just may be guilty of pulling the bandage off the scab of what the steward board was doing or had done. The order just closed the meeting with a song and prayer. NO COMMENT!

It didn't stop there. The church had a large recreation facility that had classrooms, a commercial kitchen, and a full gymnasium. Jack started a tutorial program. He met with the school's superintendent and the principals to see what guidelines he needed to visit the schools unannounced. They said all he needed was a background check (which he already had) and written consent from the parents.

We compiled a letter to send to the parents of the students in the area. We started with about fifteen students, and word got out that we helped them with their homework for an hour and fed them a meal. After their meal, they would play in the gym area, which was divided in half, so the younger children had an area to run and play while the teenage boys played basketball on half-court. We also had a room set up for those who wanted to play games.

WHO ARE THE CHRISTIANS IN THE CHURCH?

They knew we had very strict rules about cleaning behind themselves, and they weren't allowed to exit the building without the supervision of an adult. Within a month's time, we had seventy-five students. We had six teachers and two senior members who would come over and help with serving and preparing food. No funds were received from the church treasurer in support of the program. Food was provided by two couples in the church, Jack and me, and the two seniors. Fuel for the church bus was provided by a member who was a supporter of the program, and he was the only one with CDL licenses. (He also had a full-time job, and so did the rest of us except the seniors.)

The NAACP recognized a Caucasian gentleman as *Man of the Year* for his donation to the regional hospital. This donation was primarily for minorities who couldn't afford insurance or the cost of going to the emergency room. The donation was for five million dollars. His wife heard of our tutorial program. She was told about the program by one of our church members who volunteered there. She decided to come and be part of the program. She enjoyed volunteering with us. The youth also enjoyed working with her.

I am not using her name for privacy reasons. She expressed her enthusiasm about how well the program was organized and the excitement on the children's faces when it was time to eat and play. The real excitement came when the students who had such a hard time keeping up with their classes turned their grades from Ds to Bs and some As. Their attitude toward school and even themselves was so inspiring. The Caucasian volunteer stated she would like to see more programs like that in the school districts.

To our surprise, she came with a check for seventy-five thousand dollars ($75,000) to be used *strictly* for the tutorial program at the church. When it was brought before the church conference, some members became very obnoxious about how she could tell us how to spend or use "*our money.*" When the check was given, it was with a letter from the giver noting exactly the usage. After they stated that the check would be placed in the church's account and how it would be used, my husband stated he would not go to jail for them because there was a strong stipulation in the letter for the use of the money.

After stating where he stood on the use of the check, he tore the check and reminded them again that he wasn't going to jail for fraud.

Of course, there were many unhappy campers about the check being destroyed. It didn't take long before some of the same members started complaining that using the facility with so many children was destroying the church's facility. Just imagine how many churches would love to make it known that they had a tutorial ministry with that number of young children.

Needless to say, donations to the church were sufficient to cover all of the expenses of the life center. (FYI, the life center was used for Sunday school classes and other programs. It was apparent that those singing programs, talent shows, beauty contests, Sunday school classes, and using the kitchen to prepare meals for the "soup kitchen" to serve the neighborhood weren't causing any wear and tear.) Just saying!

We were blessed as far as the care of our students was concerned. We only had to expel one fellow for two weeks. Our policy states that no student is allowed to exit the building unless escorted by an adult. Our church bus driver drove his huge Harley-Davidson to the church, and one young fellow got so excited when he heard it that he ran outside. Immediately, he was called back inside and was asked by the bus driver, "Did you just violate the tutorial policy?" He dropped his head and said, "Yes, sir." Unfortunately, he was expelled for two weeks. It was a sad moment, but we had to protect the students.

Jack was able to get his schoolwork done and see if he completed it timely. After two weeks of being expelled from the tutorial classes, he came back with a different attitude. He offered to help with the younger students and made sure all areas that we used were cleaned. We were so proud of the students who seemed to not get promoted to the next grade but were making good grades after working and being so committed. They all passed to the next grade level. Congratulations were in order for the students and all the volunteers. Unfortunately, at the end of the school season, the program was shut down.

In many churches, change isn't welcome, especially if the pastor is preaching God's Word and enforcing the *Discipline* of the church. Even worse, I remember being told that we weren't welcome to live in the same city with the church members because we would be all up in their business. Oh, if only it were known how much I wanted to be back in Charlotte in my own house. If I were to say the first year was smooth sailing, I would be lying. The Lord knows I needed more than a sermon; I needed a counselor. I needed help to keep my sanity. I had never been this close to the mirror, which meant I saw and heard some awful things being said about some members and saw some actions that were a violation of the Ten Commandments. Use your own imagination.

One of the hardest parts of my first assignment as a spouse was holding my peace. I must say I have never attended a church in all my life where members felt it was okay to disrespect the pastor, even so much as trying to attack him while he was in his office at church.

When the member came into the office, he came in with an attitude. He and his clothing lit the office up with the smell of marijuana. What was his intention? Well! He thought he was going to be bold and boast that he beat up the pastor. The pastor was a medic in the army, and he knew that if he tried to come at him, what part of the body would he hit and stop him in his tracks?

You've heard it said that God has a ram in the bush. One of our friends saw Jack's car at the church and noticed who else was there, so he came in and saw that the member was going after the pastor but was stopped dead in his tracks when Jack hit him in the throat and knocked the wind out of him. He tried shouting that Jack had tried to kill him. Our friend asked what in the world made him think it was okay to try to fight the pastor. Instead, they both started witnessing to him. He later apologized.

I heard two pastors state they carried guns in their briefcases when they had church meetings. I remember how both boasted and bragged about carrying guns to their church conferences. I wonder what could've happened if my husband carried a gun, not just at meetings but while he was at church during the day. What if Jack had a gun with him when the member came to church upset because he had problems with Jack following the *Discipline* and making it known to the church conference about the checking account and the steward's reports not matching?

I am against the use of guns, but what protection does a pastor have? Would they be out of order if they tried to protect themselves? Wow! Just wondering. Of course, the incident was reversed when it was repeated by the member who was out of order. Only a few members believed him when he told them what happened. It sometimes seemed as if being a minister or pastor could be in "harm's way."

The smoke from that situation settled down quickly because a few men in the church talked with the young man about his actions. My husband will pray about an issue, and he will leave it in God's hands and move on. He knows that no one can make him feel inferior without his consent.

It may sound as if I am writing that "no good" came from our assignment at Brooklyn CME Church, but it did. We met some very dear and loving families. We are still very close to and in touch with several members there. We are still extremely close to Terry and Mildred McIntyre, their son, and his family.

I had a chance to have a silent auction to raise funds to take two young ladies to their first Christian Youth and Young Adult Conference, which is celebrated every four years. Youth and young adults come from all across the United States, Africa, and Haiti for this conference. They have various themes to discuss. That year, they were entertained by gospel singer *Mary Mary*. They had a wonderful time. At the end of the day, when we returned to the hotel, they enjoyed sitting around the pool. Oh, yes, they were in a fenced area, and my eyes were on them. They were well-mannered young ladies, and now they are grown ladies; one has a family and studied to be a life coach. She is now a traveling aide. The other young lady, I understand, has moved from the area.

I do remember there were a couple of young girls who required special attention, but I am so glad to say that one still stays in touch with us. One young lady studied to become an orthopedic surgeon, and one went back to school to study to be a pharmacist.

Several months after school closed for the summer, we started preparing for our annual conference. This is when our Carolina Regional District would meet, and different organizations in the churches would make their annual reports. At the end of the conference, the bishop would announce the names of the ministers' assignments. Some ministers may be assigned to another church or no church at all. Well! Here, we went back to Brooklyn CME, much to some's dismay.

Well, it really got steamy when Jack assigned new officers to the steward board. The previous stewards decided they weren't going to pay the assessment. The check had been made, but they didn't send it to the conference treasurer. This was intentional because they knew that a lot goes into determining the path of a pastor's assignment. We were there for a couple of months, and after the Christmas holiday, Jack received a letter in the mail saying that we had been transferred to another church. Jack was told by the order that some of the people didn't want us. Another example of *negro politics*.

So your choices are, "Do what the people want and disregard what we believe as a Christian Methodist Episcopal Church, and be gentle preaching God's Word. Know your place when you are assigned to a church. Learn your *do*s and *don't*s. Do what the people want and disregard God's Word. Pretend it's not your responsibility to know if there are any liens against the church. Don't be accountable for doing an audit. Just go with the flow and see where that will lead you. Oh, yes, please make sure that the assessments are paid. You may be there longer if you want to be there."

Believe me, the new assignment was meant to be used as an insult, but God used it as a blessing. There was a gentleman who, they felt, wouldn't accept us and would be calling to have us removed, but he, along with the church, welcomed us with open arms. That same gentleman started attending annual conferences again. Even to this day, the family still considers us part of their family. To us, it felt so heavenly and divine to drive about three hundred miles round trip to church for services and other activities.

When God calls you into the ministry, no man can stop you from preaching and doing God's will, for He will equip you.

Remember: You can cut all *the flowers, but you cannot keep spring from coming.* (Pablo Neruda)

What man meant for evil, God turned into a blessing!

Mount Calvary Christian Methodist Episcopal Church
Such a Sweet, Sweet Spirit in This Church

THE FIRST SUNDAY we traveled to Mount Airy, North Carolina, we were met on the highway by Perry, the gentleman who wasn't expected to accept us. He showed us directions to the church and stated that, when we get ready to leave, he will give us a much closer direction than the way we came. Believe me, the new assignment was meant to be used as an insult, but God used it as a blessing. Jack was assigned in the middle of a conference year. Our new assignment started in December 2005.

Upon arriving at the church, we were met with some very cordial and loving members. To my surprise, a few Caucasian families attend the church. That's what it's all about—loving thou neighbors as thou selves.

When I arrived at Mount Calvary CME Church, services started on time with our normal order of service. The young Caucasian gentleman, Nathan, played and sang a song on his guitar called "Lighthouse." (We know why a lighthouse is useful. It helps to warn mariners of dangerous shallows and perilous rocky coasts and helps guide vessels safely into and out of harbors.) The words to the song were so anointing that you could visualize what he was singing. I cried so hard, and I was so glad that the bench I was sitting on had tissues available. Oh, I can hear those words as I type. I remember the expression on his face as he was singing; it was so peaceful.

WHO ARE THE CHRISTIANS IN THE CHURCH?

When he was singing, it felt so soothing, as if God had him sing it for me. In this song, the *lighthouse* is used as a *metaphor for Jesus*. The songwriter talks about *the lighthouse on the hillside that looks over life at sea, and when he's tossed, it sends out a light that he may see. When he was in the darkness of the world, the light from the lighthouse would safely lead him o'er. But if it weren't for the lighthouse, his ship (life) would be no more.*

After service, the members told my husband that they really enjoyed his sermon. They said it was so informative that the youths were paying attention to what he was saying, and they, too, told him how much they enjoyed church. They made it known that it was hard to believe that service was over before two o'clock. Jack said, "We will be in church for about an hour or until the spirit says otherwise." He held a brief meeting to meet the members and see the officers. After the meeting, they took us out for dinner. It was an enjoyable fellowship. It was very comforting to hear how much they appreciated us for just the few hours they had already spent with us.

To us, it was a heavenly, divine three-hundred-mile round-trip drive to church for services and other activities. We were living on the east side of Charlotte at that time, which pretty much put us a long way from the main highway we needed to be near to travel to Mount Airy, North Carolina. BUT! When God calls you into the ministry, no man can stop you from preaching and doing God's will, for He will equip you. My son Butch told us the best route to travel to Mount Airy, North Carolina, and it was faster (NO MAPQUEST ON THE PHONE). LOL.

There was a member of the church who was very important to the growth and care of the church who, we were told, hadn't been to church for several months because of some grievances he had against the order and the bishop. Because of the nature of these grievances and since we were neither part of them nor in the middle of them, I prefer to say that "some things are better left unsaid."

The next Sunday, we were taken to visit him, and we introduced ourselves and where we were living at that time. I must say he was very cordial with us. My husband didn't ask why he wasn't attending church. They just talked about their lives, and he said maybe we could visit again when his wife was home. She attended a family Baptist church a few miles from where they lived.

He shared how excited he was to meet us. Jack gave him his cell number and also our house phone number. Later in the week, to our surprise, he called my husband, and they talked for a very long time. During times like that, if Jack and I were in the same room, I would usually leave so he could talk with any member, just as I would always do when a member of any of the churches called. They seemed to be enjoying the conversation because of Jack's laughter.

I have no idea what they talked about, but he was at church the following Sunday. The other church members were glad to see him as well. After services, he told my husband how much he enjoyed the service and, most of all, the sermon. The other members showed him how happy they were to see him with great big hugs and so many smiling faces, even the young children. He was like the Rock of the church. We were told he still paid his tithes and offerings.

Mount Calvary Church hosted a missionary zone meeting one Saturday. The district, Winston-Salem/Greenville, was divided into three zones to help decrease the traveling time the members would have to take to go to some meetings. Mount Calvary received such pleasant compliments for the food that was served, but most of all for the hospitality. Our youths were part of the program, and they enjoyed the workshops that were prepared for them. (I still have a picture of the youths in their missionary T-shirts.) They are all grown-up, and some have their own families now. We are still in touch with one another.

When Jack started asking about some of the people whose names were on the role that he hadn't had a chance to meet, we were offered to come up on Saturdays and stay at one of the members' homes. We felt very comfortable with the family. My reason for saying we were comfortable is that Jack never cared about staying at a member's home. We enjoyed the laughter and the fellowship with other people in Mount Airy who were church members' friends. Some of the friends would often visit the church. They were so loving and friendly as if they had known us for quite some time. Eventually, some of the "sight unseen members" trickled into services. One especially had two or three grandchildren who became active with the youth organization.

The lives of the members of Mount Calvary CME Church exemplified those of Christians. *Ephesians 4:32* comes to mind when I talk about their Christian lives.

> *Be kind to one another, tenderhearted, forgiving one another, as God in Christ forgave you.*

Another scripture they exemplified is James 1:19–20,

> *Know this, my beloved brothers: let every person be quick to hear, slow to speak, slow to anger; for the anger of man does not produce the righteousness of God.*

They are indeed children of God.

One Sunday morning, on the way to church, we had a flat tire. We were about thirty miles from the church. Jack had to put the donut tire on the car. I called the church and notified them we would be about thirty minutes late for service. Surprisingly, we were only about five minutes late. The gentleman who started back to church met Jack outside, saw the donut on the car, and asked him what he was going to do about the tire. Jack said he would need to replace it because he couldn't drive home with that tire on the car. He asked for Jack's keys. He called someone who dealt with tires, and he had him come to the church and replaced the tire. After service, our member gave Jack his keys. When Jack tried to pay him for the Michelin tire, he told Jack to get out of his face trying to pay for the tire. He and the gentleman (the one who was believed to reject us) purchased the tire. It was hard to believe they would bless us that way.

When I think of the members of Mount Calvary, I say to myself, "If only all churches reflected the characteristics of a Christian." The members of this church may have been smaller in numbers than those of the first assignment with Jack, but they had the biggest hearts. They showed love in so many ways. They may not have been able to pay the same salary that he previously received, but they met our needs in so many ways. They provided meals and a place to stay on Saturdays, so we didn't have to drive three hundred miles on Sundays, even when the Johnsons (the family home we stayed in when in town) were on vacation.

When we arrived on Saturdays, Mrs. Juanita would have a meal prepared. On Sundays, it was the norm that someone would give Jack money for us to purchase lunch or a meal on the way home. They seemed to enjoy blessing us. I guess you might say, as a songwriter wrote, "The more you give, the more He gives to you. Just keep on giving because it's really true." I really believe it was engraved in their hearts.

While we were there, Jack did some renovations to the main bathroom. The commode had a leak at the base, and the pipes were rusted under the sink. He even replaced the tile on the floor. He relocated the bathroom sink as well. Mr. Jack (the member) watched my husband as he worked in the bathroom. After completing the repairs, he told my husband what a great job he had done, and it looked as though he knew what he was doing. They both laughed because my husband always had a joke. Jack told him that being a deputy fire marshal for the state of Florida for over twenty-five years made him remember the codes and the expectations of what was the correct way to do a good job. Mr. Jack was a supervisor with a large company that did the construction for Walgreens and CVS Pharmacies. So he also knew what was needed for a job to pass inspection. Rev. Jack told him he was also doing part-time work as a private contractor with Brown and Glenn Realty Company in Charlotte.

Of course, being a contractor, he needed a truck. He met an older gentleman who was selling a Silverado pickup truck at a great deal, so he purchased it. He really liked that truck. He kept it for years. (PS. He was a bully driving that truck.) LOL.

The company Jack was contracted with decided to renovate an apartment complex and turn it into condos. So they told him to get rid of all of the stoves and refrigerators. He blessed many people with those appliances. We delivered a stove and a refrigerator to the church one Saturday. He called before we left Charlotte to ask two of the church men to meet us at church in about two hours to unload the appliances off the truck. Yes, we drove Jack's baby (the Silverado) to Mount Airy. Well, it wasn't the smoothest ride, but it was safe, and the appliances were still in one piece. The men met us at church and couldn't believe the condition the appliances were in. They moved the other stove and refrigerator and replaced them with the new ones. They said that those appliances were a blessing because there were some issues with the other appliances. One of the members stated, "The blessings keep coming."

One Sunday, close to our Episcopal District Annual Conference, Jack called a church conference after church to discuss the annual conference's plans. At this meeting, part of the agenda will consist of the reading of the pastor's church assignment. Delegates, based on the church's membership, are voted on from each church to represent the many departments, such as lay ministry (these are members who aren't ministers or pastors, such as missionaries, youths, and young adults). Unfortunately and sometimes fortunately, these delegates don't decide whether pastors will return to their present church, be assigned to another one, or be assigned a church at all. Based on the size of Mount Calvary, we were allowed to have one delegate. Perry was the delegate representing our church. The Elder was glad to see a delegate from the church because they hadn't seen a delegate from Mount Calvary for years.

At the end of the annual conference, Perry said the best part of the conference was when they announced that Jack had been reassigned to Mount Calvary. We were sitting in different areas of the conference room, but we were able to see one another, and we gave a thumbs up when they announced we were going back to Mount Calvary.

Our second year at Mount Calvary was smooth sailing. We had an opportunity to get more involved in public activities and communicate with other churches and organizations. We had members of the church who lived out of state and wanted to come home to be baptized. When they notified the church which weekend they were coming home, we planned a picnic in the park on the Saturday before the baptism. It reminded me of my childhood years when

Wesley Chapel Holiness Church in Mount Holly, North Carolina, had a baptism in the Catawba River behind the house I lived in at a very young age. I would be playing in the yard and hear some singing, and I noticed some people coming in the direction near the road that led to the river. The people were wrapped in white sheets, and a towel was wrapped around their heads. I knew they were on their way to the river for baptism. My youngest sister, Cynthia, and I would go behind them singing and stand in the crowd that was on the sidelines to watch how they were going to act after they were laid backward in the water. I was curious how long they were going to stay under the water.

At my young age, it was funny to see how they would jump up and down after coming out of the water. I knew not to let any adult see me laughing because I knew what the outcome would be. Yes, the wood part of the hairbrush on my bottom.

After completing the picnic-in-the-park plans and setting the time for the Sunday morning worship service, we notified the families and their friends of the baptism location. It was a beautiful stream that had large rocks that you could walk on. The water wasn't really deep, but it was deep enough for Jack to dip the candidates in the flowing water. The service was so anointing. When I saw the members who were baptized crying, jumping, and shouting, in my adult life, I understood what was happening with them. This time in my life, while on the sidelines witnessing a baptism, I was crying instead of laughing. I felt the presence of the Lord.

I could go on and on about how happy we were in Mount Airy at Mount Calvary CME Church. But like most good things, it came to an end when we went to the annual conference in 2008. Jack knew we were moving because Bishop Hoyt approached him prior to the end of the conference to tell him that he needed him at Reynolds Temple (which is now Christ Temple CME) in Winston-Salem, North Carolina, because they were having a problem paying their assessments. Jack was known for paying the church's assessments.

In the CME Church, I don't know how many times or at what time a pastor could choose whether they would like to remain at their last assignment (the church they were assigned last conference year) or would like to be assigned to another location. Of course, he had to say, "Yes, sir Bishop." The bishop tried to make it sound like he was getting a bigger salary, and the church had a parsonage. He even threw in fewer miles to travel. It still didn't sweeten the pot for me.

Just when I was enjoying church services again, the Mount Calvary Church families, and the city itself, I got the crushing news from Jack that we were leaving and were going to a church in Winston-Salem. I knew very little about that city. I visited the city when our church was invited to participate in programs or was at St. John CME for a conference. I never had any desire to live there.

I thought at that moment that if God wouldn't tighten my lips or punish me, I would say the d—— word and say, "Here the heck we go again." I could only let the tears flow. I know God said in *Matthew 28:20b*, *"Lo, I am with you always, even to the end of the world."*

Is it me, or have you ever felt at one point in your life that you were alone? I know God is a man Who wouldn't lie, but my selfishness at that moment blocked my heart from receiving God's Word. I wanted to stay where I felt so comfortable, like a newborn baby wrapped in swaddling clothes. The news of the move was similar to when a newborn baby is removed from the comfort and security of its mother's womb. When they are placed in the blanket, it keeps the baby calm. I felt like the baby that was delivered and flipped upside down and popped on the bottom, and I let out a big scream instead.

We were not allowed to notify Mount Calvary that we were being assigned to another church. That's just the way things "roll" in some of the CME conferences. Jack said that when he was in the Georgia conference, the bishop would discuss the new assignment with the pastors.

If I am correct, the present bishop, James B. Walker, does meet with the pastors to discuss their future assignments, especially if they will be relocating. On the Sunday following the annual conference, some churches were shocked to see a different pastor at the church. In some cases, the newly assigned pastor would have contact information for the chairperson of the steward board to possibly set up a meeting to meet the officers and discuss their expectations and any questions they may have for him. Because of our relationship with Mount Calvary, we told them we were being assigned to another church. It was heartbreaking to hear how much they were going to miss us. We promised them they would enjoy the new pastor.

Jack was invited to be the guest speaker for an afternoon program there after being assigned to another church. Several of the family's friends attended the program, and they expressed how they missed us.

Since we left, there had been two pastors assigned to Mount Calvary. The first was another male pastor who brought many family members with him. He was reassigned after serving there for several years. Many of the family members who served under him also left when he was reassigned. One thing was for sure with some people who joined the CME churches; they actually joined the pastor. If that pastor is assigned close to their home, they will join or be bench warmers at that church. The next assigned pastor was a female—the first for them. She is still there and has been for several years. We are still in contact with the family. Our conversations are centered around the families and the new babies, but never about the church.

About two years after leaving Mount Calvary Church, in the middle of November of 2009, Jack received a call from Perry to tell him that when he passed (Perry was very sick and was aware of his life timeline at this point and time), he wanted him to come and be with his mother and help her with his final arrangements. Perry had already taken care of the program; he paid a caterer for the repast and made arrangements with the mortuary. That was Perry. He and I would laugh about how we thought so much alike. We were born in the same month—November. No! We never claimed to be Scorpios, but we would laugh and say what a coincidence it was that we viewed things so much alike. LOL.

About two weeks later, Jack received the call on Sunday, November 29, 2009, from Shawn, his only sister, that our friend had passed. We went to Mount Airy immediately, as Perry requested prior to his passing. She knew how much Perry meant to Jack and me. We moved to Winston-Salem, North Carolina, after I accepted a promotion from Presbyterian Hospital in Charlotte as a supervisor in the preregistration and insurance department with Novant. We only had approximately fifty miles to travel. I tried to convince myself on the way to Mrs. March's house that I was going to be strong, not cry, and just let her talk. (It's part of my training as a hospice volunteer. I'm proud to say that several members of Faith CME were among the first Blacks to be hospice volunteers in Mecklenburg County.) NAW! It didn't happen. I tried hard to convince myself how strong I was going to be. I thought I would be okay after all the crying I had done on the way to her house. Bless be Ye, as soon as we saw each other, we both just hugged and cried until we had enough tears and mucus (snots) to drown in.

Jack allowed us to cry, and then he asked Mrs. Juanita if it was okay to pray for the two of us at that moment. She was home alone when we arrived. The family had been at the hospital waiting for news from the doctor. After receiving the news, they had time to cry and console each other. Their pastor had been informed of his passing and had already prayed for the family. As protocol and out of respect for the pastor of the church, Jack called him and shared that the deceased had made it known to the family that he wanted Jack present with his mother during the preparation of his homegoing and wanted Jack to make sure it was carried out as he had prepared. The pastor understood.

When his mother and I got our composure, she shared with Jack and me that she had called EMS because he wasn't doing well, and as he was walking toward the front of the house, he fell as soon as he reached the living room. It wasn't long before the paramedics were at the house, minutes after he fell. After working on him while at the house, they immediately took him to the hospital. He was later pronounced dead at the hospital, she said. To us, he was an immediate family member. It hurts to say we were in the Mount Airy area the day before and Jack said, "Let's go by to visit the March family."

I said, "It's not cool to drop in on people unannounced." (I was basing it on the way I think. *Bad call.*) I am sure Mrs. Juanita would have been happy for us to come by and just be with her. She talked as if she knew he was transitioning from the conversation we were having. No mother or anyone else enjoys saying that their loved one is dying.

The homegoing service was so hard for me to digest. I felt lost in space. I do remember hearing the young gentleman sing one of Perry's favorite songs, "I Won't Complain." It hurt me so much trying not to upset his mother with loud crying or sniffling. I don't remember who was sitting beside me. My husband was sitting with the ministers. All I remember is that some lady touched me and said it was time to leave. She helped me up, and when I got outside, I cried like a baby who had lost a loved one.

Elder Russell grabbed me and tried to comfort me. I remember Jack thanking him, and he told me to come and get in the car so we could go to the church's cemetery. After the committal, we went inside for the repast. When I tried to eat, I felt as though there was a big knot in my throat, and I was struggling to swallow my food. I told Jack that I just couldn't eat.

When Jack and I were preparing to leave for home, I went back to the grave and cried, saying how much I missed him and loved him still as a very loving and special friend and person. While writing this, I am so full of hurt. Tears are flowing from my eyes as I envision that moment at the grave. Jack had to really convince me why I needed to get in the car. I am glad no one commented, *"He's in a better place."* The timing would have been wrong. I probably would have said something very ugly and ungodly. Just being real about my feelings. (A little sidebar: A friend is a gift that you give yourself.) When your friend hurts, so do you. When something happens to them, you feel the pain of sadness and grief. He is remembered as being so selfless and looking out for his family. He loved his nieces and nephews dearly. We all miss him so much.

About a year later, we received a call that, once again, Mrs. Juanita had another son to pass. A graveside service was held at the church. His brother (Perry) had already purchased headstones for his siblings and mother. Here I go again, rekindling the roller-coaster emotions from missing my friend. I was reminded of a comment my mother made when one of my brothers passed away. She tearfully said, "It's hard for a mother to put flowers on her child's grave." Mrs.

WHO ARE THE CHRISTIANS IN THE CHURCH?

Juanita was struggling with a second child's death. I can't say I know how she must feel. I can't honestly, and I don't want to know. That's not a selfish comment because I would have to lose the only child I had to experience that emotion. I can only imagine. I constantly pray for God's protection around him and his whole family, even the kids who adopted him as their dad.

To this day, we are still close to the families in Mount Airy, and we stay in contact with one another.

> *True friendship comes when the silence between two people is comfortable. A good friend is like a four-leaf clover; hard to find and lucky to have.*

Reynolds Temple the End of the Road
The Dreaded Ride to Our New Assignment

Oh, the dreaded ride to our new assignment. Yes, it was closer as far as traveling was concerned, but it was farther away from my heart's desired location. When we arrived about ten minutes before to Sunday school, no one was there to greet us. We sat in the car in the church parking lot, which was at the back of the church. At that moment, you can imagine that I was very disappointed, and I felt as though I was hanging by a piece of thin thread and heading down the road for another big emotional ride.

While waiting, a gentleman pulled into the parking lot, parked near our car, and waved. He was very polite as he introduced himself as Paul Hazel. He asked my husband if he was Rev. Jack Brown Jr. He replied, "Yes, and this is my wife, Lorraine. She is comfortable being addressed as Sister or Mrs. Brown, and definitely not 'first lady.' She doesn't expect any special treatment different from the way the other women are treated in the church."

He laughed and said, "I will make it known to the congregation."

After talking to Paul for a few minutes, several members of the church arrived for Sunday school. Some were surprised to see a new pastor and his wife, and some made it known how overjoyed they were to see and meet us. (As you recall from a previous topic, I stated that sometimes the congregation's voices can help the Elder and the bishop's decisions with assignments of pastors and ministers. For those who may be confused by that statement, a pastor will always be a minister, but a pastor's status can change to that of a minister, which means they aren't pastoring a church at that time. In layman's terms, I am going to say that the pastor can be demoted to a minister [having no church assignment]. It's like a business. "Business is business, unfortunately, even in churches.")

It was time for Sunday school to begin, so Paul rang a little bell for everyone to prepare for the class. He was the teacher. He announced that he would allow enough time for the congregation to introduce themselves to the pastor and his wife and, at the same time, announced what office they hold at the church.

The membership consisted of 98 percent seniors. No children or young adults were present. One of the members stated that he has a grandson who lives in Virginia and comes to church in the summer because he spends the summer with them. After Sunday school was over, we introduced ourselves, and they introduced themselves and the office they held in the church. They were very humble and pleasant. After they introduced themselves, those who were still working made it known that some Sundays they had to work, but they always brought their tithes for the week or weeks they missed. Jack said, "Thanks for letting me know about your job. That way, I will not think there may be a medical problem or something else going on."

They treated us like very special people. We felt the same about them. It was amazing to hear the excitement in their voices about how they were looking to forward working with us. Jack met with the church for a few minutes and stated his expectations, and one thing was for sure: He made it known that there would be no meeting held on Sundays, especially after services.

Well, I looked around and started calculating how many people were employed in the church. Only five people were employed there. Of that percentage working, four were seniors (which included me). I guess I can count Jack, the pastor.

Jack was given a treasure report that showed how the members were paying their offerings. This isn't out of order because officers of the church are required to give a tenth of their earnings according to the following: *Leviticus 27:30, Proverbs 3:9, Deuteronomy 14:22–26, and the CME Discipline.* Our *Discipline* is based on the Bible and the Christian Methodist Episcopal Church's rules and beliefs. (*Just a little sidebar for your thoughts on tithes. Have you read what Matthew 23:23–24 said about the teaching or improper teaching of tithing?* You can take this time for a break to read it, read it near the end of this chapter, or easily google the synopsis of Matthew 23:23–24.)

Jack was amazed at how well the older seniors were paying their tithes. Even the workers were paying their tithes. There were other names on the roll, but they only showed up for funerals, according to the faithful members. (This isn't the first church we were assigned to where this occurred.) They didn't seem to think it was a big issue. I remember at the first assignment some of the other members would say that about members who claimed to be sick and couldn't come to church. It's amazing how and when they say, "I feel a little better," and you would either see them at the grocery store or at a funeral somewhere else, and they appear to be well. (I know this may be a sidebar here, but this action from members of churches is a sad excuse for not wanting to give praise to God for what He has done for them and has allowed them to be alive.)

Several weeks after being assigned to the church, a young man (who lived across the street from the church) asked my husband if Reynolds Temple was a private church. (The man who was renting our church's parsonage had informed Jack that the young man across the street was a drug dealer.) Jack told him, "No, anyone may come to church, including you."

He responded by saying that his mother was a member there, and he pointed to her as she approached their home. Jack introduced himself, and she softly said her name. He said it was nice meeting her and prayed that he would see her on Sunday. She came a few Sundays later. A couple of weeks later, the gentleman renting our parsonage stated that the fellow selling the drugs was locked up and that the mother had to move. The odd thing about that was that after his mother saw Jack conversing with her son, she never returned anyway. She was afraid that she would be judged by Jack, according to one of the members, who prefers that I don't identify her.

When we first arrived at the church, Jack saw the sneakers across the wires, and I said, "Well, we are in the ghetto." He said it was not necessary that it be a sign that a drug dealer was marking his territory. *Surely this is a joke*, I thought. Well, I guess he was right.

After being there for six months or more, I could see why the question may have been asked if it was a private church. You only saw the same few members come and go, except during a special program or a funeral.

For those who aren't CMEs, the churches assess certain amounts of funds based on membership. These funds are used to support the bishop's salaries, our five colleges, and other organizations, such as projects in Africa, Haiti, and here in the United States.

Mrs. Jessie Crockett and Mrs. Ruth Oree were the two who would usually organize the church programs. Mrs. Crockett was an exhorter. An exhorter is a lay speaker who isn't ordained but is certified to hold meetings, lead prayers, and evangelize. She is also an author and has written two books of Christian poems. She would reach out and invite members from other churches to take part in the programs she organized. Of course, that would draw members from those churches, who would come to support their members. Those programs were also anointed. Some were invited as guest speakers, and some were part of a play that she wrote or organized. This is the way funds were raised to help with the assessments.

Our first and second years were very successful paying our assessments. But shortly after the second conference and by the time we were getting prepared to have our programs to raise funds for our askings, Jack eulogized three of the top tithers of the church. Wow, what a big hit to the offering! I remember the pianist wanting a raise that the church couldn't afford to pay, and of all days, she wanted to meet on a Sunday. She didn't even play that day and never had rehearsals, which was a "no-no" because Jack made it plain that he wouldn't hold meetings on Sunday. She and her sister were very upset that he wouldn't have the meeting at that moment. He offered to meet her on Monday during office hours, but she refused and never came back to the church. Well, that was a saving for the struggling budget.

I remember in my younger years when many songs were sung a cappella. The beat came from the tapping of the feet on the wood floors. I still like hearing and singing songs that way, especially with beautiful harmony.

After being at Reynolds Temple CME Church for a couple of years, I transferred from Presbyterian Hospital in Charlotte to Novant in Winston-Salem, North Carolina. I took a job as a supervisor in the preregistration and insurance departments. We decided to move to Winston-Salem since Jack was pastoring there. I only had to travel about two miles to work and about three to the new church. It was very relaxing to travel such a short distance from church to home. I noticed a sweeter atmosphere living in the same town where Jack pastored in Winston-Salem, North Carolina, versus my first assignment as a minister's spouse.

The members were so kind and willing to work. Any repairs that were needed were made by some of the men of the church and my husband. There were times when the gentleman who lived in the parsonage would offer help at no charge. He was a contractor.

I remember when some shingles blew off the roof of the church, my husband climbed up a very tall ladder to the roof of the church to replace shingles that were blown off by heavy wind. It was cheaper than paying the insurance deductible. (The height wasn't a problem since he was a fireman and a fire marshal.)

Well, here we go again. Just before the annual conference, Jack eulogized two more of the top tithers. We did have a young couple who started attending church, and they paid a hefty offering when they were in attendance. Their jobs had a lot to do with how often they could attend. The church was facing hardships, but those who were still faithful tithers refused to just sit down and do nothing. The members and the pastor decided to take different expenses upon themselves and still pay their tithes. The pastor gave back over three-fourths of his housing expenses to the church, plus we paid the water bill, one member paid the alarm bill, one the energy bill, and one husband and wife paid the church's insurance. This was the only way to keep the doors of the church open.

That conference year, we were still able to pay half of the askings because we had lost two more tithers. Jack explained the hardship of the church to the higher during a church quarterly conference

WHO ARE THE CHRISTIANS IN THE CHURCH?

and how we were keeping the door of the church open by paying the bills personally. The bishop seemed to understand because that was the reason he sent Jack there. We were reassigned back to the church.

Some may ask, Why didn't you try to draw in or bring in new members? On the very same street was the largest CME Church in the city, which had more to offer members, including youth, young adults, and seniors, and many dignitaries attended there. They offered transportation as well. That wasn't a hard decision to make as to which church a person wanted to attend. On the other side of town, there were two other small CME churches on the same street, about a mile or two apart, and not too far away was another larger CME church. So there were many churches in between all of our churches that seemed to be doing well. Many years ago, the Reynolds Temple Church was a large and busy congregation. The change of leadership does make a difference.

Again, after coming back to the church, we started making plans to raise funds for the church conference year. We had a banquet that recognized certain people who have contributed so much to the churches, which included members from other local CME churches in the area. We recognize the mayor pro tem, a young girl who has received so many awards for her talent playing the saxophone. We did pretty well with the profit because the church did the catering. Many family members of the recipients purchased the twenty-five-dollar ticket to be with their loved ones. We gave them crystal platters with their names engraved on them, along with certificates. We recognized a minister's spouse, and her husband was so overwhelmed that he cried more than she did. She thought she was coming to be my guest. He said his wife was so quiet and just sat in the background, but she would help anyone in any way. I said, "That is why she received the recognition because she was so supportive of me when I was president of the Winston-Salem/Greenville spouses."

Before the annual conference, the CME churches have meetings called quarterly conferences. This is when the churches report their church's financial status to the order, which is like an area supervisor over a region. The hardship the church was having was reported to the annual conference and the quarterly conference, but to no avail. Several members spoke during the quarterly conferences of the hardships the church was facing and were told by the order that he understood.

Even to this day, I have the minutes of these meetings. But at the annual conference, it was like pouring water on a duck's back. Before to the annual conference, the higher echelon was sent a letter about the church's situation. During the annual conference, it was not acknowledged that the letter had been received. The higher (the bishop) claimed no knowledge of the hardship. I remember the hurt and disappointment my husband experienced in 2011, which forced him into early retirement in 2012.

At the 2011 annual conference in Charleston, South Carolina, Jack wasn't assigned a church. The process of confirming officers was halted by the order so he could remove my husband from the minister's examination committee (that position, according to *Discipline* Article 223.5, is appointed by the bishop, not the order). The bishop didn't remind him that he was out of order. According to our *Discipline*, the order wasn't in a position to make that call. It was done out of spite and in violation of the *CME Discipline*.

He was looking around to find someone to replace Jack, and the pastor he chose wasn't in that position for probably six months because he left the Seventh Episcopacy. That form of action again reminds me of *negro politics*.

I mentioned acts of injustice in the churches, so I want you to understand that some of you may think I'm being very harsh, and some may say that I am lying or angry. No! I am *so* far past the angry stage. Before my marriage to a minister, several ministers' spouses shared their feelings and experiences. Many sudden charges were because of the many members who didn't like change. I know from experience that my husband was charged to a church and was told by his higher not to mess up this time. That comment came about because my husband discovered that there was an unethical situation that had occurred, and he reported it to the order. He was then informed that it would be corrected. Well, I guess the best way they thought to correct it was by assigning him a new charge at that time. The "elephant in the room," which was the unethical situation

WHO ARE THE CHRISTIANS IN THE CHURCH?

and the improper way to correct the situation presented, was seen only from the higher echelon's perspective.

This retirement was a financial hardship for us because I retired in December of 2011. But we refused to let that stop us from worshiping God. I felt as if we were living under a dark cloud that obscured his life as a pastor, mainly because of personality conflicts. When it happened, I became very angry, especially at the unorthodox way it was handled. Yes, I prayed and did a lot of crying. It was so hard to believe that the higher allowed it to happen. He didn't offer to help the church financially, but instead, he kept quiet.

For years, I was bitter. Thoughts of wanting to get even flowed through my mind, but I realized that whatever I carried in my heart would blur the windows of my soul. When I looked at the biblical definition of righteousness, it *stated, "One who should act in accord with divine or moral law."* These are laws such as free from guilt or sin, morally right, or justifiable righteous decision. I knew I couldn't continue harboring anger. After constantly praying and encouraging myself to keep my eyes on God, I got through it.

I asked God for forgiveness for those evil thoughts I had because of our situation. God reminded me that I have to walk in the spirit and know that He is God, and I can't harbor anger at the same time. Truly, we don't handle anger the same way, but when it comes to God's house, we shouldn't stand by the wayside and turn our backs because we are afraid of the repercussions from men and not fear what God might do to us. After freeing myself from anger, I could truly worship God in spirit and in truth. There is an old saying that *"revenge is sweet, but forgiveness is sweeter."* Unfortunately, I was the only one suffering from carrying a bitter dislike of what happened.

Because of the passing of the higher in October 2013, a new higher was assigned to the Carolina Regional and the New York/Washington District. There appeared to be a shift in the atmosphere with the assignment of a new higher. He was very approachable. People seemed to enjoy coming to the meetings and working. The higher was very concerned about the health and wealth of the churches in the district. If he was in the area, he would visit the CME Church close by.

When he was assigned to the district, I was an officer in his cabinet. I shared a disappointment I had with an issue that occurred before he was assigned, and he felt we weren't going to work well together, mostly because I don't think he felt that what I was saying was true or had really happened. He checked the issue I shared with him and found I shared the correct information. It was nine years later, but he corrected a mistake and apologized that it happened. We both enjoyed working together.

Because of COVID-19, our conferences were held on Zoom. We really missed not being able to be with each other, but we knew what was best. It was amazing how we were able to still see each other and handle the business of the conference. As George Herbert (an English writer) was accredited for the old saying in 1640, "To him that will, ways are not wanting." Later in 1820, it was altered to say, "Where there's a will, there's a way." I say all this to say that the leadership of the conference was determined that we would continue with God's work via Zoom.

The wrath of God is being revealed from heaven against all the godlessness and wickedness of men who suppress the truth by their wickedness. (Romans 1:18 NIV)

God's Word Still Goes on Even after Retirement

Even though Jack wasn't pastoring, he still studied and prepared sermons. Yes, he could preach sermons if asked by a pastor; he just wasn't in charge of a church. The first year my husband was not pastoring, we attended Wayside CME Church in Winston-Salem under the leadership of the late Rev. Walter Funderburk.

Before the end of the annual conference year, we were directed by the higher to fellowship at Haynes Memorial CME Church under the leadership of Rev. Clarence Cox III. *It sounds funny, like being fired from a job and still being told what to do. (Just a little humor there.)* Well, that's the way the *Discipline* works. It's ironic that some articles aren't followed according to the *Discipline*, yet certain articles are. Well, to me, it's like negro politics. In the worldly saying, "It's not *what* you know but *who* you know." Please don't think I'm not familiar with the *Discipline*. I know who has the last say. Don't think that my husband doesn't remind me of the articles in our *Discipline*. But my comeback is that I am writing what I have experienced about Christians' way of life from teaching and from what they actually do, which is contrary to what they say.

When we first married, there were many occasions where acts from the higher to the higher were out of order. You read about them in the previous chapters. I gave explicit examples. There were others, but I chose not to mention them.

We followed the advice of the higher and started attending Haynes Memorial CME Church. On our first visit, the church welcomed us with open arms. I was greeted by the First Lady, the pastor's wife, to sit with her during service. It's the norm for the pastor's wife to greet another spouse who may be visiting. There was another spouse who was a member of Haynes. Her husband wasn't pastoring at that time.

During our first visit, we joined the church. We started attending the midday Bible study. During that season (Lent), they were studying from a book titled *The Bait of Satan*. Of course, we didn't have the book, but a member, Mrs. Doretha Owens, gave us one book because she said she had an extra one and she didn't want us to pay her for it. After being there for several months, Jack was asked to start teaching the midday sessions, and I became the chairperson of the senior ministry.

Later on, I was superintendent of Sunday school, and Jack was assigned to oversee the ministry to men. We both enjoyed how we were accepted at Haynes and the fun we had with the members and, of course, the pastor. Jack was asked on several occasions to preach. The members seemed to be impressed. A funny thing was that the higher was at church one Sunday when Jack preached, and he expressed how he really enjoyed the sermon that came from Matthew 14 about Peter walking on the water. Jack explained that the water was a metaphor for the distractions in our lives, which caused us to focus on them and not on Jesus. He said he never heard that scripture preached from that mindset. He offered Jack fifty dollars ($50) for that copy of the sermon. Jack thought he was joking until he pulled that money out of his pocket. They made the exchange. (This was the same higher who removed him from being a pastor for thirty-four (34) years to the status of a minister in full connection. (Again, for the non-CMEs, that means he is a minister who has pastored a church for more than two years.)

We spent several years at Haynes, along with the presence of the higher attending there. He would comment on how Jack only did what he was asked to do on the program during worship service and did not try to preach at that time. For example, if he was asked to pray or read the scriptures, he would do just that and not try to preach the prayer or the scriptures.

WHO ARE THE CHRISTIANS IN THE CHURCH?

After living in Greensboro for four years, it was time for the renewal of our lease. I told Jack I wanted to go home. Coming home allowed us to go back to my home church, Faith CME in Charlotte, North Carolina, where he was previously assigned as pastor. We moved to Belmont, North Carolina, four miles from where I was actually born, but I did attend high school in Belmont. We moved into a senior high-rise apartment complex. It was very nice in comparison with the apartment in Greensboro where we lived. The elevator was a sight for sore backs. LOL. We met some very nice people. When they learned from my sister-in-law that Jack was a preacher, they loved talking with him. We celebrated many holidays there, and Jack was always asked to pray.

Many of the women would say, "I really love hearing your husband pray."

I would say, "Yes, he's been on many homegoing services to do the prayer, even for several residents at the complex."

It was a nice place for seniors to live, but after having downsized from three, then having to in live a two- and then a one-bedroom apartment, we decided to build a home with more space. We built a home in Monroe, North Carolina, which allowed both of us to be closer to our children, grandchildren, and great-grands.

To this date, we have members from four of the churches he pastored who still call us. Jack calls them, and he has one gentleman who tells him he (Jack) knows when he needs to have him pray for him and his family. We expressed how much we missed them, but I was ready to move closer to my family in the Charlotte area. He still witnesses to them when they call and ask for prayer.

Being a retired pastor doesn't mean that your work is complete, even if you are told there is nothing available for a retired pastor in the administration. Well, for those who aren't CMEs, there are categories for retired pastors. Many are still pastoring with a different title called "*supply pastor.*" That is based on the age of the pastor.

I remind you that this is the same administration that deemed a retired pastor's input unnecessary. So if you think I am saying something that sounds contradictory. No! I am talking about the way doctrines operate in the CME Church when you reach the age of seventy (74). In our *Discipline*, Article 450 explains the use of retired pastors. Unfortunately, many pastors never pastor long enough to reach retirement age for many reasons: *(1) members, (2) not meeting financial obligations, and (3) personality conflicts.*

Being a supply pastor doesn't mean God's Word can't be just as informative and encouraging as if age or being a *supply pastor* mattered. The *supply pastor's* only concerns should be about saving souls, bringing people to Christ, and evangelizing. Being a pastor, regardless of the adjective in front of the title, doesn't stop *one* from working well with other denominations getting God's Word to lost souls.

No one is left on the sidelines at Faith CME in Charlotte, North Carolina. We have plenty of ministries, and all members are encouraged to join. Jack and I returned to Faith as a couple in 2018, and I had to move my membership back to Faith. This means that I have to get a *"letter of transfer of membership"* from Haynes Memorial because we moved back to my hometown area. This is a requirement of the *Discipline*. Simply put, my obligations (tithes, talents, and offerings) were to my home church.

With Jack being a retired pastor, he could move and attend the church of his choice. Being the former pastor at Faith, he, too, was welcomed with love. We both jumped in with both feet, working in the church. There is use for him in the church. His expertise as a retired deputy state fire marshal has saved the church from unnecessary expenses, and he is a great advisor to the trustee department.

For non-CMEs, trustees are the members entrusted to oversee and help maintain the care of the church's properties. Yes, he has preached several services since we moved back to Faith. We work as a team on the class leaders auxiliary. We contact members who may have been out of sight for several Sundays or who may just need to talk. (We are both good at talking.) He calls the truck drivers just to see how their day is going. We work as a team with the food ministry at the church. I am called to sit with one of the members when her husband has a doctor's appointment. I feel honored that they see God in me to be of assistance to them. What an honor.

If you recall from an earlier chapter, I mentioned that I told God there were three positions in a church that I never wanted to do. Well, I ended up doing one not long after I made that dumb comment, and that was teaching youth Sunday school. Well, let me tell you something funny. Our God is a jokester!

I said at a very young age that I never wanted to usher or be a stewardess in the church. God got the last say, so I became an usher and a stewardess at the well-seasoned age of seventy-six. While I am writing this book, I am seventy-seven. But being a knowledgeable Christian, I count it all joy that I can do what I do and enjoy working with the chairpersons of these two organizations. Jack is working under the leadership of a "supply pastor" and is working with a dynamic ministerial staff of great and knowledgeable ministers. Ain't God good? THERE IS ROOM AT FAITH FOR A RETIRED PASTOR. HALLELUJAH!

To my husband

Thanks for not focusing on the obstacles you faced in your ministry and keeping your eyes on the prize because God called you into it and not man. As you stated, your favorite scripture is *Psalm 31:1–3, 8 (NIV)*:

> *In you, O Lord, I have taken refuge; let me never be put to shame; deliver me in your righteousness. Turn your ear to me, come quickly to my rescue; be my rock of refuge, a strong fortress to save me. Since you are my rock and my fortress, for the sake of your name lead and guide me. You have not handed me over to the enemy but have set my feet in a spacious place.*

Scriptures That Describe the Characteristics of a Christian
Check Yourself

Lord who may dwell in your sanctuary? Who may live on your holy hill? He who walk is blameless and who does what is righteous, who speaks the truth from his heart and has no slander on his tongues, who does his neighbor no wrong and casts no slur on his fellowman, who despises a vile man but honors those who fear the Lord, who keeps his oath even when it hurts, who lends his money without usury and does not accept a bribe against the innocent. He who does these things will never be shaken. (Psalm 15 NIV)

For the grace of God that brings salvation has appeared to all men. It teaches us to say "NO" to ungodliness and worldly passions, and to live self-controlled, upright and godly lives in this present age (Titus 2:11–12 NIV)

So I say, live by the spirit, and you will not gratify the desires of the sinful nature. For the sinful nature desires what is contrary to the Spirit, and the Spirit what is contrary to the sinful nature. They are in conflict with each other, so that you do not do what you want. (Galatians 5:16–17 NIV)

My dear brothers, take note of this: Everyone should be quick to listen, slow to speak and slow to become angry, for man's anger does not bring about the righteous life that God desires. (James 1:19–20 NIV)

Will you be able to say, "Yes, I am a Christian," based on the above scriptures?

Summation

THE SONGWRITER CLAY Evans wrote the words, "When I look back over my life and I think things over, I can truly say that I've been blessed. I have a testimony." It's sad to say that it has taken years to see and know that I know that God has been good to me, even when I just didn't think He had any part or anything to do with the road I traveled to be seventy-eight years old.

Trying to believe He was there wasn't easy because I had so many doubts. Of course, that was my fault because I was so impatient with the Lord and everyone else. But God made it known that He wasn't on my schedule. Well, I am going to tell a very bad joke here. You've seen on the news that when kids get into trouble, they blame it on their parents. Well, here goes a good one. I am going to say that when our mother told us to do something (all but the youngest child; she was spoiled), she meant for it to be completed by the time it got out of her mouth. No joke! So I am not even crazy enough to say it was because of her that I am or was impatient.

I am not using my youth experience for my *unbalanced* Christian walk because 2 Timothy 2:15 (KJV) clearly states the following: "*STUDY to shew thyself approved unto God, a workman that needeth not to be ashamed, rightly diving the word of truth.*" I didn't know how to study for my own understanding as a child. I didn't have the materials available when I was younger.

As a child, I watched adults and compared their actions to what they said. I found it to be confusing and the opposite of what I was taught in church. The *why* in me was because I didn't know if there was a godly explanation for why they were doing acts contrary to God's Word. Children depended on their parents, Sunday school teachers, and ministers to explain the scriptures and Jesus's parables, and I never ever, as a child, heard anyone explain that metaphors are a way of explaining the scriptures.

I also learned when I was in my sixties that there were many adults who had never heard the word. A *metaphor* is a figure of speech in which a word or phrase is applied to an object or action. It is not literally applicable; it was used as a cross-reference to common terms. Examples: *The Lord is my Shepherd*. This means He's a spirit, and we are the *sheep*. We are in the animal kingdom, but we don't have white wool on our bodies or graze in the grass. That was used to give a *visual* idea of how important we are to God. He watches over us like a shepherd watches over his flock of sheep. Another good example is, "*God will move our mountains*." Those *mountains* are issues in our lives that are blocking our growth in His Word. So that's why we have to study to show ourselves approved. As I stated earlier, I rarely hear a sermon from the New Testament.

Maybe you have a *why* person in your home or your life. Give it some thought to make sure they aren't just trying to challenge you but really need your understanding. We heard the story of a daughter questioning her mother about a certain way she was preparing food. The mother responded by saying, "My grandmother and mother always did it this way." The child still wanted to know why. The mother was stunned because she really had no other explanation or really took time to ask her mother or grandmother (if available) why. Think of *why* as not being a bad question if you are confronted with it.

In your walk with Christ, please remember the following two quotes:

> *Only some of us learn by other people's mistakes. The rest of us have to be the other people.* (Eleanor Roosevelt)

> *Wisdom is the principal thing; therefore get wisdom: and with all thy getting get understanding.* (Proverbs 4:7 KJV)

WHO ARE THE CHRISTIANS IN THE CHURCH?

Remember to "dream of the person you would like to be, but remember that God won't waste the person you are" (unknown).

This I do know. My past can't be used to discourage me. May God bless you, and I hope that something I said will be a blessing to you.

God bless!

When I Say I Am a Christian
(Carol Wimmer, 1988)

When I say, "I am a Christian,"
I'm not shouting, "I've been saved!"
I'm whispering, "I get lost sometimes
that's why I chose this way."

When I say, "I am a Christian,"
I don't speak with human pride;
I'm confessing that I stumble,
needing God to be my guide.

When I say, "I am a Christian,"
I'm not trying to be strong;
I'm professing that I'm weak
and praying for strength to carry on.

When I say, "I am a Christian,"
I'm not bragging of success;
I'm admitting that I've failed
and cannot ever pay the debt.

When I say, "I am a Christian,"
I don't think I know it all;
I submit to my confusion,
asking humbly to be taught.

LORRAINE McCULLOUGH-BROWN

When I say, "I am a Christian,"
I'm not claiming to be perfect.
My flaws are far too visible,
but God believes I'm worth it.

When I say, "I am a Christian,"
I still feel the sting of pain.
I have my share of heartache,
which is why I seek God's name.

When I say, "I am a Christian,"
I do not wish to judge.
I have no authority.
I only know I'm loved.

About the Author

LORRAINE MCCULLOUGH-BROWN was born in a small city southwest of Charlotte, North Carolina, called Mount Holly, North Carolina. She was the tenth child in a family of twelve children. To this day, she only remembers living with only four siblings. After three of her brothers graduated from high school, they joined the military; the oldest brother worked in construction along with her father. All the girls went to college.

Lorraine's mother was a PK (a.k.a. preacher kid). When the last five siblings were in high school, their father and oldest brother started working out of state with the construction company for many years. Their mother had no problem with disciplining them. What rules were made *stayed. She didn't waiver from them.* Lorraine can remember those rules so well.

Listed below are some of the rules:

- No listening to rock and roll (rhythm and blues) music on Sundays
- No playing baseball/softball on Sundays (Basketball wasn't that popular.)
- Only color in a biblical coloring book
- Not attending Sunday school or church wasn't an option.

They had to participate in church programs as well. During their young years, the church had books called *Children's Catechisms*, which they had to learn. It consisted of the Lord's Prayer, the Ten Commandments, the Beatitudes, and the Twenty-Third Psalm. Yes, they had church assignments just like in public school.

After graduating from Reid High School in Belmont, North Carolina, she attended a historically Black College and university at North Carolina Central University in Durham. There, she studied sociology because she wanted to study people's behavior and their reactions to certain issues in their lives and life itself. A very common definition she would use was, "What makes a person *tick*?"

Lorraine is the mother of one biological son, Robert LaVelle "Butch" Baker. His father passed away at a young age. Presently, she is married to Rev. Jack Brown Jr. With their marriage, there are two sons—her son, Robert, and Therus; and four daughters—Jackie, Cherlania, Carmita, and Kelle. They have nineteen grands and sixteen great-grands. It's a joy to be with them whenever they can.

Lorraine has never regretted the fact that she had to attend church as a youth. Even at seventy-eight, she is still learning, and it's a blessing.

Printed in the USA
CPSIA information can be obtained
at www.ICGtesting.com
CBHW021516011124
16780CB00001BA/15